The Imagination of Loving

It was very probably this sweet-tasting property of the observed thing in itself that was mainly concerned in Ralph's quickly-stirred interest in the advent of a young lady who was evidently not insipid. If he was consideringly disposed, something told him, here was occupation enough for a succession of days. It may be added, in summary fashion, that the imagination of loving—as distinguished from that of being loved—had still a place in his reduced sketch.

(*The Portrait of a Lady*) [1]

The Imagination of Loving

by Naomi Lebowitz

Henry James's Legacy to the Novel

Wayne State University Press

Detroit, 1965

To Al

ᵉ᷾ Acknowledgements

I would like to thank Jarvis A. Thurston, Joseph H. Summers, and Stanley Elkin who read this manuscript in its original thesis form. Each gave me his own unique and invaluable criticism and encouragement.

I also wish to thank the following for their kind permission to quote from works to which they hold the copyright: The Viking Press, Inc., *Phoenix,* by D. H. Lawrence; Albert Mordell, *Literary Reviews and Essays,* by Henry James; Houghton Mifflin Company, "The Lesson of Balzac" in *The Question of Our Speech,* by Leon Edel (later reprinted in *The Future of the Novel*); Charles Scribner's Sons, *Autobiography, Art of the Novel,* and *Notes of a Son and Brother,* by Henry James, also excerpts from *The Letters of Henry James,* ed. Percy Lubbock, and the following books by Henry James: *The Ambassadors, The American Scene, The Better Sort, The Golden Bowl, The Ivory Tower, Notes on Novelists, Portrait of a Lady, The Sacred Fount, A Small Boy and Others, The Wings of the Dove* (copyright 1908, 1909, 1913, 1914 Charles Scribner's Sons; renewal copyright 1936, 1937, 1941, 1942 Henry James), and Prefaces to *Roderick Hudson, The American, Portrait of a Lady, The Princess Casamassima, The Spoils of Poynton,* and *What Maizie Knew* (copyright 1907, 1908 Charles Scribner's Sons; renewal copyright 1935, 1936 Henry James); Paul R. Reynolds, Inc., *The Future of the Novel* by Henry James; J. M. Dent and Sons, Limited, *The House of Fiction,* by Henry James; Rupert Hart-Davis, Limited,

Acknowledgements

Literary Reviews and Essays, by Henry James; Wayne State University's *Criticism,* "The Sacred Fount: An Author in Search of his Characters," IV (Spring, 1962), by Naomi Lebowitz, slightly rewritten as Chapter VII of this book; and the *Sewanee Review,* "Magic Metamorphosis in *The Golden Bowl,*" LXXIII (Winter, 1965), by Naomi Lebowitz, slightly rewritten to become Chapter VIII.

N.L.

ᷔᷓ *Contents*

ᓚᔆ *Preface*

There are still many critics, like Frank O'Connor, who would agree with H. G. Wells's description of the James novel as "a church lit but without a congregation to distract you, with every light and line focused on the high altar. And on the altar, very reverently placed, intensely there, is a dead kitten, an egg-shell, a bit of string." [2] Wells is censuring what seemed to him the thin quality of James's realism. O'Connor describes the reader who, "glaring over his shoulder . . . perceives in astonishment that James is much more concerned with his private arrangements than with the value of the loot and that, in fact, he is quite content to use any old gimcrack chair or pot as a stand-in. The arrangements are impeccable and rigorous, but at times they resemble those of a magpie of genius rather than those of an artist." [3] Though the perspectives of a critic like Yvor Winters seem worlds apart from those of Wells, both complaints about James's style tend to the same conclusion. James, asserts Winters, was master of "the most unsound narrative technique antedating Joyce, Miss Richardson, and Mrs. Woolf . . ." [4] Winters is devoted to the traditional physical, social, and ideological supports of plot and theme. James's particular moral sensibility, which he shared with his characters, "was a fine, but a very delicate perception, unsupported by any clear set of ideas, and functioning, not only in minds of very subtle construction, but at the very crisis in history at which it was doomed not only to be almost infinitely rarefied but finally to be dissolved in air." [5] Because Winters yearns for fixed conclusions, just as Wells yearns for fixed opinions, he deplores in James the beginnings of fragmentation of the natural order and integration of plot, character, thought, and word, a condition that seems to "plague" the modern novel.

Those admirers of James who are concerned with the novelist's social responsibility, critics like Lionel Trilling and Irving Howe, feel the need to expose the roots of his realism. Trilling and Howe, in important essays on *The Princess Casamassima* and *The Bostonians*,[6] assume that these novels show a James sensitive not only to social manners but also to social conscience. Quentin Anderson, in a strong and impressive book, supplies James with a base deeper than the social soil by emphasizing the legacy of his father's energetic religious consciousness which provided a natural moral groundwork upon which he could build his major novels:

> What this meant to the novelist was that he did not have to cobble up for himself a set of inclusive values and beliefs about man and his destiny, as did Hawthorne and Melville. He did not so much borrow as continue to employ a mode of vision which had colored his childhood.[7]

Anderson's thesis can make certain claims for validity, but when he makes the last great novels rise to apocalyptic heights, I think we must question the direction of his lead. Whatever emblems and allegories James incorporated into these thickly textured novels we have to treat on aesthetic rather than metaphysical terms.[8] The difference between James's dramatized morality and the hortatory moralities of his father and brother is a difference in substance as well as form.

Actually the James of the "major phase" is only burdened by these claims for social or religious sensitivity. He continually defined his moral vision out of his own novelistic preferences and creations. James used objects of dogma from the altar of religion and masks and costumes of role from the stage of society, but he used them more often for symbolic dimension than for realistic texture, cautionary or celebrative purpose. Critics may find it worthwhile to trace James's concepts of personal freedom, American spontaneity, and the corruption of institutional civilization to a transcendental and anti-transcendental inheritance, to the very personal emphases of Henry James, Sr., and we might even suppose that the paternal creation of a moral system to fill the vacuum of a faded Calvinism [9] applies to the son too.

But James was as little interested in historical motivation from the past as he was in the apocalyptic promise of the future. In the case of Hawthorne, the *lack* of American social tradition could be deplored because James was speaking about the tribulations of the American *novel,* and he was far more interested in the welfare of his characters than he was in the salvation of mankind. The description of the last novels which Christof Wegelin offers: idealizations of "social beauty" (Mme de Vionnet in *The Ambassadors*), "high spiritual beauty" (Milly Theale in *The Wings of the Dove*), and the fusion in the union of Maggie and her Prince in *The Golden Bowl*,[10] in which the progressive and apocalyptic intention is denied, seems more satisfying than Anderson's contentions, while still reflecting the concerns of Henry James, Sr James's subjects preached his realism through their dynamic human relationships.

James was a novelist of realism, but his realism did not spread from Jane Austen's fixed social base of manners, nor from George Eliot's inalterable moral or ideological stances. He learned much from these two masters for his preferred realism had the moral conscience at its center, but it was not the conscience of comedy or philosophy. It was neither inherited, predetermined, finished, nor complacent. It loosened itself from social convictions and was committed instead to human relationships. If James's base seems fragmented, it is because it is not fixed. His morality is formed out of the constant exposure of a sensitive character to the possibilities of engagement. Many readers have been troubled by supposed ambiguities or open ends in his major novels. Often James's apparent ambiguity is a way of showing us that morality must be continually redefined since human hearts must be continually earned. Because of this emphasis, in one instance, the adultery of Chad Newsome and Mme de Vionnet in *The Ambassadors* may in truth be termed a "virtuous attachment," while, in another, that of Charlotte Stant and the Prince in *The Golden Bowl* may be symbolic of truly deeper personal deceptions concerning the quality of love. The moral realism of James does not fragment life, but even when framed by a fairy tale, credits life's complexities.

From *The Portrait of a Lady* (1881) through *The Sacred Fount* (1901), and in the major late novels, James became progressively absorbed by the idea of using the relationship between individuals, itself so variable, as a measure of morality and a strategy of structure. He was well aware of the many forms the novelist's world could take: "The house of fiction has . . . not one window, but a million." [11] But despite his theoretical support of a variety of approaches and subjects, James, like most practitioners, tended to evolve judgments and evaluations of novels from his very particular blend of irony and sympathy. He was concerned with defining *his* kind of novel, what we might term the novel of personal relationship. As he grew older, James seemed to move farther and farther away from any devised system of thought and morality found in his father and to become more and more engaged in expressing his central novelistic commitment to the individual lives of his characters, so different from the philosopher's primary concern with universals.

The natural and primary relationship which James used as the technical and moral center of his "relational" novels is the love relationship between major characters, that between Isabel Archer and Ralph Touchett, Isabel and Gilbert Osmond in *The Portrait of a Lady;* that between Merton Densher and Kate Croy, Densher and Milly Theale in *The Wings of the Dove;* that between Strether and Mme de Vionnet, Chad and Mme de Vionnet in *The Ambassadors;* and that between Maggie Verver and the Prince, the Prince and Charlotte Stant, and Maggie and her father in *The Golden Bowl.* When the characters of major consciousness themselves explore their relationships, they can make moral judgments based on the contrast between honest and full communion and the communion that is built on secrecy, on information without love, or on the influence of unchanging objects and pictures. When we say that these relationships are formed in freedom we imply that James has disengaged his reader from the traditional novelistic bases of social or dogmatic stands and forced him to concentrate upon individualized commitments in all their dynamic development.

Neither place nor doctrine names his major novels, but rather fluid symbol. Those novelists who are otherwise closest to him, George Eliot and Jane Austen, serve by contrast as good pointers to this distinctive characteristic. The title *Middlemarch* implies that human life is determined by and closely involved in a particular society, a particular moral code; *Pride and Prejudice* suggests that human connections are made by the adjustment to firm moral societal poles of conduct; but *The Portrait of a Lady, The Wings of the Dove,* and *The Golden Bowl,* carry the weight of the tense struggle of the personal relation against ritual. *The Golden Bowl,* James's most mature novel, is formed, on both the aesthetic and ethical fronts, out of an uncompromising exposure of its characters to the possibilities of this struggle. So exposed, their infancy grows to marriage, their romance to a larger realism, and picture to symbol.

But the bonds between characters rest, in turn, upon a certain kind of commitment of author to subject. My first chapter, based upon James's most insistent critical assertions, attempts to show that for James a novelist's capacity to project the proper moral weight depends upon the amount and nature of "felt life" in the novelist himself and upon the direction of his moral imagination. The second chapter is concerned with the manner in which relationships structured the James novel. Since the general thesis of this book is most fully exemplified in *The Portrait of a Lady, The Wings of the Dove, The Ambassadors,* and *The Golden Bowl,* novels which are closely bound in theme and development, discussion will center upon these works, though reference will, of course, be made throughout to other instances outside these novels. Chapters III and IV measure the quality of mind and passion that the James characters must have in order to relate meaningfully and deeply. Chapter V exposes the hazards of dogma and the old moralities, as James saw them, to both novelist and character. Chapter VI suggests a new perspective in the interpretation of *The Sacred Fount:* as a critical blueprint for a future novel, the book playfully teases and tests James's favorite concepts of composition and the necessary felt life between character and author. The chapter on *The Golden Bowl,* in which the fullest trajectory of a James heroine is traced, points up that assumption of compositional power by the major character that was sketched in *The Sacred Fount.* The last chapters attempt to evaluate James's legacy to the modern novel. A review of James's own attitudes to the "old" novel, particularly French, English, and American, and of his accounts of failure and success, limitation and possibility, allows us to project his relevance for the "new" novel. Henry James cannot escape being a central figure in modern debates over the future of the novel, and his own optimism and example, richer than ever for our time, can help us to answer the protests of Wells, O'Connor, and Winters.

~§ I *Introduction*

"And what is the honest lady doing on that side of the town?" [1]

Henry James

One of Henry James's best known stories about artists is a compact study of his obsessive interest in the connections between life and art. He establishes a direct interdependence between marriage and the "Figure in the Carpet." The narrator of Vereker's story, who typically sees himself as a "coerced spectator," [2] questions briefly but tellingly the effects of his own lack of ethical engagement upon his aesthetic sensibilities: "Was the figure in the carpet traceable or describable only for husbands and wives—for lovers supremely united?" [3] Earlier, he had dryly observed of his friend's annoyingly private activities:

> Mrs. Erme's death brought Corvick straight home, and within the month he was united "very quietly"—as quietly, I seemed to make out, as he meant in his article to bring out his *trouvaille*—to the young lady he had loved and quitted. [4]

Whatever the irony directed against the prying critic, there is no questioning the direct relationship between the discovery of an artistic secret and the consummation of an engagement of love. Vereker himself had admitted that marriage might be a decided help for aesthetic revelation. If for no other visible reason, remarks the narrator concerning the fortunate lovers, "poor Vereker's inner meaning gave them endless occasion to put and to keep their young heads together." [5] The James artist is regularly denied normal relationship in life, but he has the great privilege of granting it to others. As marriage is the most manifest symbol of deep relationship, James gives it presumptive credit. His final proof, however, lies in the reality of the relationship itself and not in its appearance, in its substance and not in its ritual.

Commitment to human relationship, morally sanctioned not necessarily by the laws of society but by the measure of its own strength and depth, is James's supreme ethical concern, and he sees it as the natural and central concern of his special aesthetic form of expression, the novel.[6] Life and the expression of life thrive on the richness or starve on the poverty of the same commitment, and nothing so clearly reflects the painful recognition of artistic waste in Gabriel Nash (*The Tragic Muse*) and the painter of "The Madonna of the Future" as does that of the long absence of genuine human engagement in Strether and Marcher. The deep analogy between human and artistic engagement is playfully, but nonetheless seriously, probed in the intriguing tale "The Story In It." James here brilliantly puts forth the vital centers of both his criticism and fiction: real life, like the life of the novel, cannot be rounded in untried innocence; real life, like the novel's life, demands relationship, and relationship demands commitment, and commitment demands painful exile from the first Eden before entrance into the second. That is what the realistic Voyt (who, like Gabriel Nash, does not, even while speaking wisely, escape the Jamesian brush of irony) means to say when, after defining the deep and dark areas of the novel, he slyly asks: "And what is the honest lady doing on that side of the town?" [7]

As so often when he wants to cut through the false purity of untainted romance and idealism, James here makes use of the French tone for his apparently cynical norm. Voyt says of the Gallic artists:

> "They do what they feel, and they feel more things than we. They strike so many more notes, and with so different a hand. When it comes to any account of a relation say between a man and a woman—I mean an intimate or a curious or a suggestive one—where are we compared to them?" [8]

And when Maud Blessingbourne, who makes a fatal separation between life and art, complains of the monotony of so much sin in the French novel, Voyt points out that her interest "is in something different from life." [9] " 'Ah, not a bit,' " protests Maud. " 'I *love* life—in art, though I hate it anywhere else. It's the poverty of the life those people show, and the awful bounders, of both sexes, that they represent.' " And Voyt responds:

> "Oh now we have you! . . . To me, when all's said and done, they
> seem to be—as near as art can come—in the truth of the truth. It
> can only take what life gives it, though it certainly may be a pity
> that that isn't better. Your complaint of their monotony is a com-
> plaint of their conditions. When you say we get always the same
> couple what do you mean but that we get always the same passion?
> Of course we do. . . . If what you're looking for is another, that's
> what you won't anywhere find." [10]

Because we know that James's own complaints about the realistic-
naturalistic French novel, center not so much on the ground or on
the conditions covered as upon the way they are covered, upon the
meager centers of consciousness which serve as registers, we can
reasonably assume that James grants Voyt's argument a large measure
of critical sanity.

As the dialogue proceeds, the story focuses sharply upon a more
particular interest, the intersection of the moral and aesthetic problems of innocence. Maud begins:

> "Well, I suppose I'm looking, more than anything else, for a
> decent woman. . . . Women aren't *always* vicious, even when
> they're—"

Voyt interrupts:

> "When they're what?" . . .

And Maud explains:

> "When they're unhappy. They can be unhappy and good."

To this Voyt responds:

> "That one doesn't for a moment deny. But can they be 'good'
> and interesting?" [11]

A further dimension comes to light when we remember that James
had suggested in his criticism of *Madame Bovary* the possibility
that a heroine could be both "bad" and uninteresting. For Flaubert
and Zola, innocence is more an aesthetic than a moral concern. They
do not define their moral position by the Jamesian use of characters

who represent varying degrees of ethical intensity and possibility. Nor is there, in a central character, a moral evolution that would shape and develop the open, good, and untaught soul. We must understand that Voyt's extremism is caused by a passionate belief that, in both life and art, the "romance" of Maud, that demands a false "purity," means the renunciation of real relationship, and that the renunciation of real relationship means the end of life and the death of the novel: " 'If a relation stops, where's the story? If it doesn't stop, where's the innocence?' " [12] This is the problem that faced the creator of Milly Theale and Maggie Verver. Maud herself, unwilling to accept Voyt's syllogism, is a Maggie who never grows up. In real life Voyt could present a possible story to Maud, a story depicting a real relationship between Maud's hostess and himself, but the story could not be written by Maud because it could not be seen by her.[13] The artist whose romantic vision refuses to recognize the dynamism of relationship as the life of the novel will give to the world a stillborn work. Maud's opponent finally has this to say about relationship:

> "The subject the novelist treats is the rise, the formation, the development, the climax, and for the most part the decline of one. And what is the honest lady doing on that side of the town?" [14]

This is Voyt's ultimate retort, and, if we understand that "honesty" means "untested innocence," it is James's as well.

ᴥ§ II *Felt Life: Relationship Begins at Home*

Vision and opportunity reside in a personal sense and a personal history, and no short cut to them in the interest of plausible fiction has ever been discovered.[1]

Henry James

1.

At the root of James's criticism and of his fiction lies the conviction that "in life without art you can find your account; but art without life is a poor affair." [2] The life that, for James, must be projected in art, that has vital connections with the cultivation of "felt life" [3] in the author himself, must be reflected in the consciousness of characters in the novel. What ultimately bothered James about a novelist like Flaubert was his stingy projection of parental concern and the subsequent impoverishment of his creations. When James complains that Frédéric Moreau (*L' Education sentimentale*) is an insufficient register for a novel's central intelligence,[4] he is correcting Flaubert both technically and morally, for while the shallowness of Frédéric's insight (a concomitant of Flaubert's use of unremitting irony) seriously limits the range and depth of the novel's dramatic potentiality, it also reflects a personal limitation. To some critics James may seem to be on dangerous footing, but he dared to suppose that it is because Flaubert's own spring had been tampered with [5] that his fictional hero remembers as the best time of his life his first pathetic and uncertain sexual attempts in a brothel. By contrast, James's Strether gains depth and breadth by recognizing waste in his life through the absence of passion. Strether's remembrance, the picture of Mme de Vionnet and Chad on the river, detaches itself from implications of societal immorality when he discovers a deeper relational morality. Frédéric's remembrance, as he hears the taunting laughter of whores as life's most beautiful song, provokes

[*21*]

the bathetic collapse of his intelligence. While Strether cuts all the strings of time to guarantee that the sense of life, its meaning (if consummation is no longer possible), may remain in the Present, Frédéric sums up years in a few pages, ironically because those years *can,* in their emptiness and deterministic repetition, be so easily accounted for. But he does not quit the Past. That is the only time there is. Frédéric's sensibility must inevitably remain escapist as it inevitably remains meager.

Here, and habitually, James defined himself by explicit or implicit opposition to other novelists he both admired and censured. His use of sensitive people in relationship as structural center of the novel was a deliberate answer to novelists like Flaubert whose ideal center was "nothing" or like D'Annunzio who reduced art by isolating it from the process of living. His criticism, and his fictional pieces on artists which culminate in *The Sacred Fount,* are permeated with the conviction that "felt Life" is the necessary bridge between author and character, character and character, and between the tones that enrich these relationships, the romantic ("the things that . . . we never *can* directly know; the things that can reach us only through the beautiful circuit and subterfuge of our thought and our desire") and the real ("the things we cannot possibly *not* know, sooner or later").[6] The novelist must stand upon this bridge, looking at times to one side, at times to the other, for the sake of compensating the claims of characters and tempers. More often than critical purists would like to admit, James concentrated upon the needs, intentions, and potentialities of the man on the bridge before talking of the bridge itself, for the Flaubertian ideal of absence from the scene, of making the falling tree sound without witness or even woodsmen, was not James's. The stream of his novel demanded a reflection of sympathy from the author as witness (though not, of course, the physical intrusion), for the verification of its life flow.

But we ought, at this point, to turn away from the water, for while James preferred stream metaphors to express relational involvements between his characters, when he spoke of those between author and subject he preferred the more solid terms of the soil:

> The question comes back thus, obviously, to the kind and degree of the artist's prime sensibility, which is the soil out of which his subject springs. The quality and capacity of that soil, its ability to "grow" with due freshness and straightness any vision of life, represents, strongly or weakly, the projected morality. That ele-

[22]

ment is but another name for the more or less close connection of the subject with some mark made on the intelligence, with some sincere experience.[7]

Since the capacity for art was always for him dependent upon the capacity for life, it is to be expected that relationship begins at home with cultivation of the primary engagement between author and subject. In one of the central paragraphs of "The Art of Fiction" James wrote:

> There is one point at which the moral sense and the artistic sense lie very near together; that is in the light of the very obvious truth that the deepest quality of a work of art will always be the quality of the mind of the producer. In proportion as that intelligence is fine will the novel, the picture, the statue partake of the substance of beauty and truth. To be constituted of such elements is, to my vision, to have purpose enough. No good novel will ever proceed from a superficial mind; that seems to be an axiom which, for the artist in fiction, will cover all needful moral ground. . . .[8]

Like Keats, James closely associated the energy of Art (for Beauty and Truth) with the condition of the artist's mind (negative capability). But because for Keats the poet, identifying "the substance of Beauty and Truth" in the projected poem depended more upon the powers of unfelt life than upon those of felt life, we might, in the case of James the novelist, alter the formula for artistic preparation from negative to metamorphic capability. For both the poet and novelist the absorptive power of Beauty depended upon the ability of the viewer's mind to remain in "uncertanities, mysteries, doubts." But James was such a lover of consciousness that he preferred to emphasize the capacities for compositional reaction and direction in the novelist. In addition, the negative capability is essentially aesthetic and amoral, whereas the Jamesian capacity must be morally guided. The difference between the poet and novelist in the face of the subject can readily be seen by contrasting the following quotations, first of Keats, second of James:

> The excellence of every art is its intensity, capable of making all disagreeables evaporate, from their being in close relationship with Beauty and Truth. Examine "King Lear," and you will find this exemplified throughout. . . .[9]

To be completely great, a work of art must lift up the reader's heart; and it is the artist's secret to reconcile this condition with images of the barest and sternest reality. Life is dispiriting, art is inspiring; and a story-teller who aims at anything more than a fleeting success has no right to tell an ugly story unless he knows its beautiful counterpart. The impression that he should aim to produce on the reader's mind with his work must have much in common with the impression originally produced on his own mind by his subject. If the effect of an efficient knowledge of his subject had been to fill his spirit with melancholy, and to paralyze his better feelings, it would be impossible that his work should be written. Its existence depends on the artist's reaction against the subject; and if the subject is morally hideous, of course, this reaction will be in favor of moral beauty.[10]

James is not comfortable with depersonalization of any kind. His impatience with the dispiriting barrenness of many of the naturalistic novels reflects his disgust at their lack of the metamorphic capability. The "romance" of the mind which allows the free and sympathetic debate of possibilities between author and subject (and real choice on the part of character) was deliberately snubbed by the naturalistic variety of realism. When the novelist is not open to his subject, he willfully quarantines Beauty from Truth. The subject itself shrinks to an object and offers the narrowest bounds for relational exploration.

The mind of James in Maggie Verver, a cooperation that illustrates the fullest working of sympathetic control, plays at a far distance from the suppressive objectivism of the naturalistic mind. Maggie's ultimate competence to direct and shape her reactions and those of others, to consummate her own relationships in the world of *The Golden Bowl,* is an assumption of compositional power from the compositional felt life behind her in the real world. For James, the separation of the felt life of the artist from that of the subject and the subsequent surrender of judgment and consciousness in a character, reduced the novel to painfully small proportions. The novelist, like James's greatest heroines, must take the risk of involvement. He must, in a sense, set a good example for his characters.

It is obvious that, of all art forms, the widest reflection of felt life can be attained by the novel, a form which prides itself upon its expansive capacity and uses the most extensive connections between the real world and its own:

Here we get exactly the high price of the novel as a literary form —its power not only, while preserving that form with closeness, to range through all the differences of the individual relation to its general subject-matter, all the varieties of outlook on life, of disposition to reflect and project, created by conditions that are never the same from man to man . . . but positively to appear more true to its character in proportion as it strains, or tends to burst, with a latent extravagance, its mould.[11]

Because the form and choice of subject reflect a felt life that selects (the moral imagination), James became progressively more demanding about the fullness of subject. He grew impatient with the merely fanciful. Of his own short story "The Altar of the Dead" he wrote:

But the thing is a "conceit," after all, a little fancy which doesn't hold a great deal. Such things betray one—that I more and more (if possible) feel. *Plus je vais,* the more intensely it comes home to me that solidity of subject, importance, emotional capacity of subject, is the only thing on which, henceforth, it is of the slightest use for me to expend myself. Everything else breaks down, collapses, turns thin, turns poor, turns wretched—betrays one miserably. Only the fine, the large, the human, the natural, the fundamental, the passionate things.[12]

But the "fine, the large, the human, the natural, the fundamental, the passionate things" are only neutral terms without the posted life behind them:

The house of fiction has in short not one window, but a million—a number of possible windows not to be reckoned, rather; every one of which has been pierced, or is still pierceable, in its vast front, by the need of the individual vision and by the pressure of the individual will. These apertures, of dissimilar shape and size, hang so, all together, over the human scene that we might have expected of them a greater sameness of report than we find. They are but windows at the best, mere holes in a dead wall, disconnected, perched aloft; they are not hinged doors opening straight upon life. But they have this mark of their own that at each of them stands a figure with a pair of eyes, or at least with a field-glass, which forms, again and again, for observation, a unique instrument, insuring to the person making use of it an impression distinct from every other. He and his neighbors are watching the same show, but one seeing more where the other sees less, one seeing black where the other sees white, one seeing big where the other sees small, one seeing coarse where the other sees fine. . . . The spreading field, the human scene, is the "choice of subject"; the pierced aperture, either broad or balconied or slit-like or low-browed, is the "literary form"; but they are, singly or together, as nothing without the posted presence of the watcher—without, in other words, the consciousness of the artist. Tell me what the artist is, and I will tell you of what he has *been* conscious. Thereby I shall express to you at once his boundless freedom and his "moral" reference.[13]

The novelist selects his soil, cultivates his own garden, and is responsible for his crops. For all his "felt" burden of national consciousness, James was convinced that the Fates, Time and Place, could be ruled by the felt life within.

2.

Much of what James has to say about the relationship of a novelist to his work serves as a protest against the French naturalists or cultists of the "pure" craft. This protest is strong despite his appreciating what the French contributed to the modern novel, principally "lessons" to the English mind on the relativity of conventional morality in literature and in the impressiveness of documentary accumulation. James believes that the naturalistic ideal of excluding authorial passion and judgment from an artistic center of consciousness represents a terrible deprivation. He recoils from the chill of the Goncourt portrait because art should be, of all things, "amiable." Lest we think of this adjective in its most superficial connotation, James follows his protest with a deeper and difficult definition:

> It is not amiable when it is narrow and exclusive and jealous, when it makes the deplorable confession that it has no secret for resisting exasperation. It is not the sign of a free intelligence or a rich life to be hysterical because somebody's work whom you don't like affirms itself in opposition to that of somebody else whom you do; but this condition is calculated particularly little to please when the excitement springs from a comparison more personal. It is almost a platitude to say that the artistic passion will ever most successfully assuage the popular suspicion that there is a latent cruelty in it when it succeeds in not appearing to be closely connected with egotism.[14]

"Amiability" is the end product of the artist's metamorphic intelligence working upon subject, and the term's smooth surface hides deceptive turbulence.

We must pay particular attention to the subtlety of James's definitions of the artistic process when he speaks of the productive relationship of artist to subject in words which call to mind that aesthetic blandness of neo-classical criticism. Like "amiability," the recurrent measures of "taste" and "saturation" [15] only appear mild. Both terms weigh the quantity and quality of felt life behind the artistic expression; both terms refer directly to the intensity of involvement of artist with subject. This is why they are so often present in James's criticism of the French novelists. The French example was a threat to the novel's metamorphic capacity and to the novelist's metamorphic capabilities. The taste that selects and the amiability that is effected in tone are major props for the business of artistic transformation. When the naturalists ignore them they subject the novel to a crude scorching. James justifies one of his favorite paradoxes, that refined reality is morally more honest in literature than unrefined reality, at the expense of the school of Zola:

> Go as far as we will, so long as we abide in literature, the thing remains always a question of taste, and we can never leave taste behind without leaving behind, by the same stroke, the very grounds on which we appeal, the whole human side of the business. Taste, in its intellectual applications, is the most human faculty we possess, and as the novel may be said to be the most human form of art, it is a poor speculation to put the two things out of conceit of each other. Calling it naturalism will never make it profitable.[16]

To carry the paradox further, the exclusion of taste from the process of selection, rather than encouraging the unusual, the interesting, or even the natural, fosters instead the conventional. In the same review of *Nana,* James observed:

> The figure of the brutal *fille,* without a conscience or a soul, with nothing but devouring appetites and impudences, has become the stalest of the stock properties of French fiction. . . . He [Zola] is welcome to draw as many figures of the same type as he finds necessary, if he will only make them human. . . .[17]

James is not complaining about the subject exposed, but about the mind behind it, about that mind's refusal to stir the crucible of dramatic involvement. It is not the crudity of cannibalism that bothers James, but the absence of zest for its flavor: "It is not . . . choice of subject that has shocked us; it is the melancholy dryness of . . . execution, which gives us all the bad taste of a disagreeable dish and none of the nourishment." [18] Immorality marks not the subject but the failure of the artist to engage himself in the subject. The lack of taste is not just a handicap; it is fatal:

When you have no taste you have no discretion, which is the conscience of taste, and when you have no discretion you perpetrate
books like "Rome," which are without intellectual modesty, books
like "Fécondité," which are without a sense of the ridiculous,
books like "Vérité," which are without the finer vision of human
experience.[19]

Instead of refining the necessary life experience into art experience,
Zola has deliberately allowed the common in life to possess and control him. He has made a fateful choice: "If you insist on the common
you must submit to the common; if you discriminate, on the contrary, you must however invidious your discriminations may be called,
trust to them to see you through." [20]

Balzac at least gives us the impression of being "personally over-
taken by life, as fairly hunted and run to earth by it," [21] and he uses
science *for* art. But Zola protects himself from deeper penetration
into life by holding that science "applies *us*," [22] can predict our
actions as well as prepare them, and Zola must accept the consequences of moral and artistic impoverishment. In his praise for
Germinal, l'Assommoir, and *la Débâcle,* James acknowledged that
Zola's strength lay in his epic scope, in his sociological eye riveted
on the crowd, but James's attachment to the needs and the worth of
the individual case made Zola's apocalyptic vision, in which the
moral position became didactically separated from the drama, seem to
him a superficial poetic romanticism which failed in its responsibility
to the central subject. The heroism of the single suffering soul must
always supersede that of a struggling social evolution. James repeatedly implies that the novelist must not allow the common in reality
to master him, but must himself master reality in the artistic process
by a dramatic infusion of the romantic, "that beautiful circuit and
subterfuge of our thought and our desire." While American writers
too often translated reality into a rigid romance (a form which, instead of exploring relationship's "romance," paradoxically limited
relationship for the sake of personifying morality), the French naturalists lost the dramatic potentialities of the real when they excluded
the Jamesian romance altogether.

That the necessary involvement of the artist's felt life with that of
his subject is a moral relationship for James, as free and bold in its
play as that of character to character, is even more strongly evidenced
when James turns from the naturalism of Zola to the sweeter fields
of Sand's idealism:

She was a sentimentalist of a very high order, but she was not a moralist. She perceived a thousand things, but she rarely in strictness judged; so that although her books have a great deal of wisdom, they have not what is called weight.[23]

The weight of which James speaks is the product of the forceful fusion of felt life in the artist with a fictional center of consciousness. We must remember that "amiability" and "taste" are not passive terms but shape, determine, and reflect the strength of the connection between conscience in artist and conscience in subject. It is for the tenuousness of this relation in Sand's work that James censures her idealism just as he had, from another angle, blamed Zola's naturalism. Zola misuses reality by failing to refine it, while Sand misuses it by overrefining it:

George Sand's optimism, her idealism, are very beautiful, and the source of that impression of largeness, luminosity and liberality which she makes upon us. But we suspect that something even better in a novelist is that tender appreciation of actuality which makes even the application of a single coat of rose-colour seem an act of violence.[24]

Nor does her passion for the anatomy of love bring her any closer than Flaubert to the human:

If other things come and go with George Sand, amatory disquisition is always there. It is of all kinds, sometimes very noble and sometimes very disagreeable. Numerous specimens of the two extremes might be cited. There is to our taste a great deal too much of it; the total effect is displeasing. The author illuminates and glorifies the divine passion, but she does something which may be best expressed by saying that she cheapens it. She handles it too much; she lets it too little alone. Above all she is too positive, too explicit, too business-like; she takes too technical a view of it. Its various signs and tokens and stages, its ineffable mysteries, are all catalogued and tabulated in her mind, and she whisks out her references with the nimbleness with which the doorkeeper at an exhibition hands you back your umbrella in return for a check.[25]

The vivid contact between author and subject, character and character, the energetic meeting which determines the moral discretion of the novel, seems to James to be noticeably absent in much of the French literature that he admires for other qualities. Sand's fluidity, Zola's naturalistic detail, Balzac's picturesque immersions, Flaubert's incisiveness, the sensuality of Baudelaire's vision and the animalism of Maupassant's are symptomatic of an artistic activity and initiative which make a healthy contrast to the growing atrophy of the English novelistic tradition. But at the same time, these very qualities tend to deny the priority of commitment to personal relationship that James aims for in the novel; they stunt the novel's dimension when they avoid sensitive registers or when they render impossible the flexible development that relationship demands.

In Turgenev, James found a beginning of that balance of the romantic and the real that he sought. Turgenev easily matches Sand's fluidity, but at the same time, his object is

> that of finding an incident, a person, a situation, *morally* interest-ing. This is his great merit, and the underlying harmony of his apparently excessive attention to detail. He believes the intrinsic value of "subject" in art; he holds that there are trivial subjects and serious ones, that the latter are much the best, and that their superiority resides in their giving us absolutely a greater amount of information about the human mind.[26]

He has the sensuous fineness of the French, but he has in addition "an apprehension of man's religious impulses, of the *ascetic* passion, the capacity of becoming dead to colours and odours and beauty, never dreamed of in the philosophy of Balzac and Flaubert." [27] Here, with deep critical insight, James pushes the concept of negative capa-bility back to its most literal level. He is attracted by the notion that while the French naturalists and realists pretend to show us the depths of man's despair and boredom, and the French idealists and romanticists add the heights of man's expansive sensibilities, they are working with only surface because they suppress the spiritual inde-pendence of their characters. To realize the great potentiality of his form the novelist must attach to its aesthetic dimension an ascetic dimension, a dimension which implies not the removal of judgment but its active moral presence in character; not determinism but moral choice; not meaningless amoral surrender, but significant moral re-nunciation. Because Flaubert split off the romantic from the real, his asceticism was false. The intense pain and anguish which James de-scribes, arose in the soul of Flaubert from terrible sublimation of the romance of his spirit to the narrowing realism of a bourgeois vision of experience, a sublimation which could be controlled artistically only through an unmitigating and dispassionate irony. Irony and the

romantic scene (the "perversion" of the Jamesian "romantic") were
Flaubert's escape routes from the human.[28] Flaubert himself, who
identified his martydom with that of St. Polycarp, constantly pro-
claimed that his style was a defense against the ugliness of life.
Instead of bringing to art a positive felt life, he came to the novel to
escape from life, either by mocking its ugliness or by seeking historical relief. The radical difference in temperament between James and
Flaubert is reflected in their aesthetic motivations and directions. The
fullest realization of their antithetical natures and attitudes comes in
lines like this in letters from Flaubert to Louise Colet: "Think of
me now: having constantly to be in the skins of people for whom
I feel aversion." [29] Or, "I am turning toward a kind of aesthetic
mysticism." [30] It is merely perverse, or perhaps just superficial, to
call James, with Flaubert, Ben Jonson, and James Joyce, a "saint" of
literature on the grounds that he wrote in spite of himself, that he
loved literature not wisely (morally) but too well (aesthetically).[31]
James himself writes:

> Let Flaubert always be cited as one of the devotees and even, when
> people are fond of the word, as one of the martyrs of the plastic
> idea; but let him be still more considerately preserved and more
> fully presented as one of the most conspicuous of the faithless.
> For it was not that he went too far, it was on the contrary that
> he stopped too short.[32]

Shut out from the discovery of that balance between the romantic
and the real which comes with the granting of wider sensitivity to
character, Flaubert controlled the conflict from his own distanced
isolation and eked out the perfect chilly spoils. The romantic became
the safety valve for his own personal relief; he could not use it for
the shaping, the deepening of the real.[33] James comments:

> The "gift" was of the greatest, a force in itself, in virtue of which
> he is a consummate writer; and yet there are whole sides of life
> to which it was never addressed and which it apparently quite
> failed to suspect as a field of exercise. If he never approached the
> complicated character in man or woman—Emma Bovary is not the
> least little bit complicated—or the really furnished, the finely
> civilized, was this because, surprisingly, he could not? [34]

In a book like *L'Education sentimentale* the split between the romantic and the real is manifest: "It is in the background and the acces-
sories that the real, the real of his theme, abides; and the romantic,

the romantic of his theme, accordingly occupies the front." [35] In this design, the real can only mock the romantic.

The same failures, of involvement and balance between author and subject, mark the efforts of the Goncourts. Again we find James facing us with the effects of a divorce between the creator and his expression:

> They represent the analysis of sensation raised to its highest powers, and that is apparently the most original thing that the younger French imaginative literature has achieved. But from them as from Gustave Flaubert the attentive reader receives an indefinable impression of perverted ingenuity and wasted power. The sense of the picturesque has somehow killed the spiritual sense; the moral side of the work is dry and thin.[36]

Such moral emaciation is a part of the general stylistic martyrdom of Flaubert. In a letter to T. B. Aldrich James writes:

> The torment of style, the high standard of it, the effort to say something perfectly in a language in which everything has been said, and re-said—so that there are certain things, certain cases which can never again be attempted—all this seems to me to be wearing them all out. . . .[37]

If, James suggests in a discussion of Daudet, we (from the English, and by extension American, standpoint) tend to find the sensory world through a moral and metaphysical orientation, the French reverse this process.[38] James exercises his Anglo-American bias to protest against the reduction of moral exploration to a stagnant picture:

> To stir the reader's moral nature, and to write with truth and eloquence the moral history of superior men and women, demand more freedom and generosity of mind than M. Feuillet seems to us to possess. Like those of most of the best French romancers, his works wear, morally, to American eyes, a decidedly thin and superficial look. Men and women, in our conception, are deeper, more substantial, more self-directing; they have, if not more virtue, at least more conscience; and when conscience comes into the game human history ceases to be a perfectly simple tale.[39]

Where the sensory world crowds out the moral, relationship and drama are flattened, and story is narrowed to tale. Whenever the potentialities of the relational novel, as James saw it, are threatened by the closing of the famous authorial windows we are sure to hear a strong critical complaint. If Maupassant's "mansion" is "compact," it is compact at a very high price, the price of showing to the reflective side of human nature "a perfectly dead wall." [40] For James, genuine compactness is made of more transparent stuff. In an imagined offhand address which carries suggestive resentment against the sacrifice of the reflective conscience in character to the naturalistic demands of the material world, James says to Maupassant:

> So much the better for you, if you wish to describe life without it. The strings you pull are by so much the less numerous, and you can therefore pull those that remain with greater promptitude, consequently with greater firmness, with a greater air of knowledge.[41]

But the ease of Maupassant's puppet show mastery is a slothful ease, the ease of the mere picturesque. When authorial manipulation replaces natural dramatic movement of character, the sacrifice of possible moral depths and discoveries is too great for James to accept.

His criticism of Balzac is far more complex. James's vigorous admiration for that author depended upon the contrast of Balzac's great powers of immersion, his shameless personal dips into art, "the very spirit and secret of transmigration" [42] with the cautious objectivity of the Flaubertian school. But the rendering of even Balzac's great "life" freezes too often to the picturesque, and Balzac himself tends too readily to see character as an extension of thing. Balzac cannot hold steadily to the drama of growing conscience in character and he breaks the power of immersion by scientific reporting. At times James's resentment against the caricatured relationship between author and subject in Balzac's work resembles a Marxist protest against the cash nexus of all bourgeois relationship:

> The imagination, as we all know, may be employed up to a certain point in inventing uses for money; but its office beyond that point is surely to make us forget that anything so odious exists. This is what Balzac never forgot; his universe goes on expressing itself for him, to its furthest reaches, on its finest sides, in the terms of the market.[43]

Though accepting the risks of immersion raises Balzac above Zola and Maupassant, in the long run Balzac shares in the French penchant to limit novelistic depth by substituting temperment for conscience.[44] The rich uses of conscience are credited by James to the English masters, particularly George Eliot. The "tasteless" preference of temperament to conscience brings Balzac into the camp of Zola: "He has no natural sense of morality, and this we cannot help thinking a serious fault in a novelist. Be the morality false or true, the writer's deference to it greets us as a kind of essential perfume." [45] The English masters, on the other hand, have given off a fair share of this perfume: "They care for moral questions; they are haunted by a moral ideal. This southern slope of the mind, as we may call it, was very barren in Balzac. . . ." [46] Balzac's vision is not finely enough focused on the descent from Paradise, on the conscience of moral loss and gain shaped on the slope away from Eden. It is on this slope that all of James's great goddesses of consciousness, especially Isabel Archer and Maggie Verver, measure and are measured. In place of this evolving moral judgment, the romantic Balzac gives us "an aesthetic judgment" and too often "duplicity is more picturesque than honesty." While James points to the great contrast between Balzac and himself, he is also implicity revealing the distance between Lucien de Rubempré and Isabel Archer. The James character is ultimately beautiful through "a magnificent sacrifice, a magnificent devotion, a magnificent act of faith" whereas the Balzac actor prefers to be picturesque by a "magnificent lie, a magnificent murder or a magnificent adultery." [47]

What we may repeatedly assert is that for James, the preference on the part of the novelist for the mere picture of drama over the actual drama of genuine engagement is not just a limiting fancy but an immoral act, immoral to the same degree that unfunctional, undirected, sexual allusion is in the literature of love. A diet of "pigments and sauces" leaves the reading public "morally stranded and helpless." [48] There is a direct connection between the almost exclusively sensual diet of a Gautier and a Baudelaire and their amoral digestion. While Baudelaire revels in the sensuality of a rotting corpse, Gautier can look at beggars sunning themselves in Rome and "see nothing but the fine brownness of their rags and their flesh-tints—see it and enjoy it for ever, without an hour's disenchantment. . . ." [49] For James this kind of detached sensuality presented as much a dead end to the novelist as the bestial reductions of Maupassant. The relational novelist's vision needs to see the mockery behind "picturesque squalor," needs to make moral judgments of what has been lost to human glory since the Fall and what can be regained. Since we have the knowledge of good and evil we must act upon it and react to it. But James saw Baudelaire's concern as an "inordinate cultivation of the sense of the picturesque"; [50] the meaning or use of things and ideas for human life is secondary.

When James sought a contrast to the moral picturesque he turned to his own great American master Hawthorne. The use of Hawthorne to reveal Baudelaire's moral superficiality carries ironic implications, for in both his pieces on Hawthorne, James had stressed the "picturesqueness" of Hawthorne's puritanism. And it is, after all, to the orchards of Europe that the American innocent goes to bite into the apple. But when James writes of Emerson's lack of education in Evil, he uses Hawthorne for his corrective. The blank wall to moral complication, which Maupassant's house featured, becomes a blank wall to sin and its consequences in Emerson's mansion:

> Hawthorne's vision was all for the evil and sin of the world; a side of life as to which Emerson's eyes were thickly bandaged. There were points as to which the latter's conception of right could be violated, but he had no great sense of wrong—a strangely limited one, indeed, for a moralist—no sense of the dark, the foul, the base. There were certain complications in life which he never suspected. [51]

If there is one thing that clearly differentiates the fallen from the unfallen state it is that in the latter state Evil is known as an outside force, as allegory; after the Fall, Evil is interiorized, experienced in the human soul. When Baudelaire tries to make Evil picturesque, he is drawn to the structure of the Edenic scene without concerning himself with its spirit:

> He knew evil not by experience, not as something within himself, but by contemplation and curiosity, as something outside of himself, by which his own intellectual agility was not in the least discomposed, rather, indeed (as we say his fancy was of a dusky cast) agreeably flattered and stimulated. [52]

It is Hawthorne who is the real master of experiential Evil:

> A good way to embrace Baudelaire at a glance is to say that he was, in his treatment of evil, exactly what Hawthorne was not— Hawthorne, who felt the thing at its source, deep in the human consciousness. Baudelaire's infinitely slighter volume of genius apart, he was a sort of Hawthorne reversed. [53]

Because, in James's view, Baudelaire's sense of Evil does not come out of his felt life, it is not deep: " 'Le Mal?' we exclaim; 'you do yourself too much honour. This is not Evil; it is not the wrong; it is simply the nasty.' " [54]

When the moral weight is drained from our conception of Evil we are left with the dregs of moral impressionism. The equation points again and again to the pronouncement which, in the best James tradition, allies life and art: that the picturesque, while having its own pleasant virtues, is immoral when accepted as the end of art or life. It means that the finer vision, the deeper relationship is being glossed over. James's willingness to pass freely from the poetic vision to the novelistic vision might indicate the degree of his absorption in the moral world of the novel. Yet there is no confusion of meaning in the analogy. In the world of James it is as impossible to talk of artistic effect without considering the moral reference at its source as it is to separate craft from subject. The stylishly casual approach which talks of morality as "Miss Edgeworth's infantine heroes and heroines talk of 'physic' " [55] is both immature and incomplete. The moral sense which infuses subject matter with weight, and which really determines the selection of subject as well, is

> simply a part of the essential richness of inspiration—it has nothing to do with the artistic process and it has everything to do with the artistic effect. The more a work of art feels it at its source, the richer it is; the less it feels it, the poorer it is. People of a large taste prefer rich works to poor ones and they are not inclined to assent to the assumption that the process is the whole work. [56]

3.

The French faults represent only one side of James's critical position. Our lessons on the novel are not complete before we consider the faults of the English and American writers who counted for him. It is no better to stay huddled on what James calls the southern side of the purgatorial mountain of art than it is to isolate oneself on the northern side. [57] Eventually the novel's south, or moral depth, and the novel's north, the fine rendering of aesthetic perception, are bound roundly by the course of the sun, the artist's own flexible vision, which moves from east to west. It is the same vision that binds the romantic and the real, picture and drama, and ultimately character to character. James insists on having the novelist and his center of consciousness, or character, submit to the shaping of both the aesthetic and ethical exploration, to the changing perceptions, recognitions, judgments that are registered through expanding metaphors. This is the double change in consciousness which forces readjustment in relationship, which brings together the picture of it (the aesthetic) and the truth of it (the ethical). The novelist of relationship, and those characters through which he composes, must find and face the subject on all slopes of the mountain. Just as James turns around and around Maggie's situation for the sake of maximum discovery, so Maggie, once she takes up the challenge of definition and adjustment, tracks down her problem from all angles. This persistent circling is the same critical process which James uses in examining the work of other novelists. We might note here, that if, as Ezra Pound suggests,[58] James freed himself in his later criticism from a kind of provincialism, the stylistic heightening and intensification which mark the late novels and criticism is where true progression lies. James's basic critical tenets, his principles and judgments of authors, though moderated and expanded from time to time, remain remarkably constant and enable us to pass without frequent chronological reminders from one essay to another.[59]

While James felt, on the one hand, that the French devotion to the morally picturesque threatened the relational novel, he pointed out that the English and American novelists endangered the relational novel by failing to anchor the moral and the metaphysical in the sensory world: "We have doubtless often enough the courage of our opinions . . . , but we have not so constantly that of our perceptions." [60] This is a subtle distinction, but it tells us that we have fatally split the areas of romance from the areas of the real. We hope that opinion has the appearance of perception just as we hope that the picturesque romantic has the appearance of the true. In a letter to Howells, for the sake of clarifying the American problem, James speaks well of those French naturalists and realists we have seen him censure:

> There is nothing more interesting to me now than the effort and experiment of this little group, with its truly infernal intelligence of art, form, manner—its intense artistic life. They do the only kind of work, to-day, that I respect; and in spite of their ferocious pessimism and their handling of unclean things, they are at least serious and honest. The floods of tepid soap and water which under the name of novels are being vomited forth in England, seem to me, by contrast, to do little honour to our race. I say this to you, because I regard you as the great American naturalist. I don't think you go far enough, and you are haunted with romantic

phantoms and a tendency to factitious glosses; but you are in the right path. . . .[61]

If at one stage James directed the moral possibilities of the genuine romance toward correcting the limitations of the false real, now he uses the honesty of even that limited view of the real to correct the dangers of false romance, to banish the "romantic phantoms." From this angle, Maupassant is to be admired. James refuses, as his growing heroines must learn to refuse, the easy judgment. Definition, both aesthetic and moral, is not opinion but perception. Now it is the English and American novelists, rather than the French, who fail to have the courage of their perceptions, to write naturally from them:

> We are apt to be misled by some convention or other as to the sort of feeler we *ought* to put forth, forgetting that the best one will be the one that nature happens to have given us. . . . There is a whole side of our perceptive apparatus that we in fact neglect, and there are probably many among us who would erect this tendency into a duty.[62]

At their best, writers like Zola and Maupassant display both the courage to write straight from their own given premises and the persistence to follow through a line of consistent exploration no matter the direction, and this is a kind of artistic honesty. The shy false sense of "duty" that forces an evasion of the demands of this exploration is but a "betrayal of a sacred office." [63] Like the isolating subservience to the picturesque, the isolating avoidance of ugliness and evil is artistically immoral. It is the novelist's great privilege to be at once "philosopher and painter," [64] roles that must fuse in the dramatic process. Only through constant and energetic interweaving of the Good and the Evil with the Ugly and the Beautiful is the novelist exercising his special privilege.

James saw the tendency to retreat from the straight line of perception largely as a problem of the contemporary novelist. But he was able, on the same grounds, to criticize some of the English masters, notably Trollope whose great crime is that he "gives his fiction away," that he deprives the novelist "at a stroke of all his standing room" by arbitrarily adjusting his narrative to the reader's whim.[65] This compositional play, rather than reflecting a bold confidence, is symptomatic of the general diffidence of the English novel to reveal unpleasant truths to its public, in contrast to the French:

In the English novel (by which of course I mean the American as well), more than in any other, there is a traditional difference between that which people know and that which they agree to admit they know, that which they see and that which they speak of, that which they feel to be a part of life and that which they allow to enter into literature. . . . The essence of moral energy is to survey the whole field. . . .[66]

The beginning of artistic morality is, from this point of view, the registering of the real, of those things we cannot afford not to know.

Yet when James looks at the strengths rather than the weaknesses in the works of novelists who influenced him, it is the English novel which satisfies most fully his sensibility. The diffidence of the English novel can be corrected; it is essentially a superficial cautiousness. The French novel may be superior in "audacity, in neatness, in acuteness, in intellectual vivacity, in the arrangement of material, in the art of characterizing visible things," but the English novel is "more at home in the moral world," [67] and the moral world honors a deep perception of character, of changing relationships, the very essence of James's novelistic focus. We remember that the novelist whose center is the morality of relationship must connect the "beautiful circuit and subterfuge of our thought and desire" with those "things we cannot possibly *not* know." It is in the circuit of romance that moral judgment is refined, and James's preference for the English novel is really a preference for that positive moral position (though not, we have seen, the merely forceful opinion), which eventually conquers irony and cynicism (though the artist might work toward his moral position through these attitudes):

The feeling of life is evidently, *de part et d'autre,* a very different thing. If in ours, as the novel illustrates it, there are superficialities, there are also qualities which are far from being negatives and omissions: a large imagination and (is it fatuous to say?) a large experience of the positive kind. Even those of our novelists whose manner is most ironic pity life more and hate it less than M. de Maupassant and his great initiator Flaubert. It comes back I suppose to our good-humor (which may apparently also be an artistic force); at any rate, we have reserves about our shames and our sorrows, indulgences and tolerances about our Philistinism, forbearances about our blows, and a general friendliness of conception about our possibilities, which take the cruelty from our self-derision and operate in the last resort as a sort of tribute to our freedom.[68]

This is not a smug defense of comfort in the English novel. Any reader of James's criticism knows that this freedom is his *sine qua non* for the novel's future as a form, and freedom starts in the strokes of the mind, not in those of the pen. The seemingly free sense-exposures of the French represent freedom of the pen only; they point to minds enslaved too often by the non-commitment of an unrelenting and apparently amoral irony:

> The love of sport, the sense of decorum, the necessity for action, the habit of respect, the absence of irony, the pervasiveness of childhood, the expansive tendency of the race, are a few of the qualities . . . which ease us off, mitigate our tension and irritation, rescue us from the nervous exasperation which is almost the commonest element of life as depicted by M. de Maupassant.[69]

James asks of Flaubert's work: "How can art be so genuine and yet so unconsoled, so unhumorous, so unsociable?" [70] The insistence on significant moral weight in the novel is not divorced from, but closely allied to, this conception of freedom. Moral weight in James develops not from dogmatic message or pronouncement, rigidly maintained distance, but from flexible sympathy and identity, relational play. From this viewpoint, even Stevenson has more positive moral weight than many of the French writers because the

> part of life which he cares for most is youth, and the direct expression of the love of youth is the beginning and the end of his message. His appreciation of this delightful period amounts to a passion, and a passion, in the age in which we live, strikes us on the whole as a sufficient philosophy.[71]

If experience is only adventure it does not contain the melancholy of dry executions. And if Tom Jones is not a deeply conscious register, "he has so much 'life' that it amounts, for the effect of comedy and application of satire, almost to his having a mind." [72] Unlike Flaubert, who dreaded, hated, and determined his "alien skins," Tom Jones's creator is so "handsomely possessed of a mind—has such an amplitude of reflexion for him [Tom Jones] and round him that we see him through the mellow air of Fielding's fine old moralism, fine old humour, and fine old style, which somehow really enlarge, make every one and every thing important."

When James turns to those novelists whose moral weight is more overtly philosophical he is jealous for both the life and the form of the novel, but again, he is glad for the passion. Some of his most important comments on this aspect are expressed in his criticism of George Eliot, the novelist to whom, despite their obvious differences, he felt perhaps the greatest debt, and for whom, often, he felt the deepest admiration. An ideological base for the novel, a base which modern critics of the novel as various as F. R. Leavis, Edwin Muir, Christopher Caudwell, Lionel Trilling, and Irving Howe have at one time or another recommended, demands a commitment that James could appreciate. He recognized that Eliot often drew a convincing life from the fixed moral base of those of her novels which functioned ideologically. But it was perhaps the fear that philosophy and history compete with relational flexibility in the novel that led James to remark of Eliot's work:

> It sets a limit, we think, to the development of the old-fashioned English novel. Its diffuseness, on which we have touched, makes it too copious a dose of pure fiction. If we write novels so, how shall we write History? [73]

If her characters are at times flattened by idea, still, "the cooling draught of ethical purpose" [74] allows us to care. When she succeeds in properly backing the particular, the individual case, so sacred to James, with the general philosophical case, she is a consummate novelist:

> Her preoccupation with the universe helped to make her characters strike you as also belonging to it; it raised the roof, widened the area, of her aesthetic structure. Nothing is finer, in her genius, than the combination of her love of general truth and love of the special case. [75]

It was always, whether in life or art, for the retention of the individual case in the midst of universal pressures that James worked. In a moving condolence letter (which he could have written to all his heroines at their moments of crisis) he pleads with Grace Norton to avoid the temptation of blurring the lines of life: "Don't melt too much into the universe, but be as solid and dense and fixed as you can." [76]

It is this retention of individual density which marks George Eliot at her best. In spite of its dead areas, the world of George Eliot demonstrates what authority can reside in the novel which springs from significant and directed felt life. It is always to this source that James points us. The Sainte-Beuve in James was fascinated with the way Eliot's particular choice of life affected her art, the way her ostracism from social acceptance led her to "a kind of compensatory earnestness." [77] But she has the great gift of the best novelists, the ability "to live with high consistency for herself" that allows "her nature all its chances." [78] And this, of course, in art, means the determination to drive one's story with maximum power and with consistent direction.

What endangered Eliot's work, especially her later novels, was a loss of balance between perception and reflection, and only then did her novels fail in life.[79] She yielded too often to the temptation to see reality as reflection, abstraction. This is a fault in *Romola,* but James's appreciation of that novel, despite the belief that it is "less a work of art than a work of morals" reveals how important for the substantial novel he considered moral weight: "I declared to myself that much should be forgiven it for the sake of its generous feeling and its elevated morality." [80] The firm moral source of Eliot's strength allows the inevitable and fated relation between thought, deed, and guilt in her novels to anchor the individual case, but her limitations of dramatic imagination made it difficult to release the individual from social determination. That is why James calls Eliot a conservative in morals and aesthetics, despite her great contribution to a strong novelistic tradition:

> In morals her problems are still the old, passive problems. . . . What moves her most is the idea of conscience harassed by the memory of slighted obligations. Unless in the case of Savanarola, she had made no attempt to depict a conscience taking upon itself great and novel responsibilities.[81]

It is James who assumed the task of freeing morality from societal or philosophical attachment and commitment and of allowing it to depend instead upon the quality of the individual act of relating. Eliot does not always grace the "middle field" where "morals and aesthetics move in concert." [82] She is forced by her nature to compromise with the old tradition; and the individual case of renunciation, of painful moral reevaluation and expansion is frequently sacrificed to the old *deus ex machina* of an arbitrary "optimism":

> I know few things more irritating in a literary way than each of her final chapters,—for even in *The Mill on the Floss* there is a fatal "Conclusion." Both as an artist and a thinker . . . our author is an optimist; and although a conservative is not necessarily an optimist, I think an optimist is pretty likely to be a conservative.[83]

James would have preferred the tempests of the heart to the floods and earthquakes that prevent Maggie from being "left to her own devices." [84] Where in Eliot was Isabel Archer's painful turning back to a once-traversed purgatory? Even the fairy tale tonality of *The Golden Bowl* tempers its final optimism with the recognition of the necessity of a continual earning of marriage. Ultimately, Eliot's reflective tendency, her conservatism, and her forced optimism account for the loss of dynamism in the individual commitment to relationship, for the sense of the good static picture rather than the moving connection. James himself speaks of her superiority in "drawing attitudes of feeling" rather than "movements of feeling." [85] James, who never flinches from the growing pains of his major characters, is disturbed by the facile portrait of Dinah Morris, by the substitution of pictorial for deep psychological motivation:

> If by nature she had been passionate, rebellious, selfish, I could better understand her actual self-abnegation. I would look upon it as the logical fruit of a profound religious experience. But as she stands, heart and soul go easily hand in hand. I believe it to be very uncommon for what is called a religious conversion merely to intensify and consecrate pre-existing inclinations. It is usually a change, a wrench. . . .[86]

When Eliot is willing to work thoroughly with the individual case she can be highly convincing. James is full of admiration for the rounded portrait of Gwendolen, perhaps the most influential fictional character for his own great heroines. But again, when reflection in *Daniel Deronda* gets in the way of perception, we get the dead characters of the Jewish half of the book.[87] Constantius, the major spokesman in James's enlightening dialogue on *Daniel Deronda* clarifies Eliot's failure by claiming that she has substituted the aesthetic for the dynamic examination of character: "Jews in general take themselves much less seriously than that. They have other fish to fry. George Eliot takes them as a person outside of Judaism— aesthetically. I don't believe that is the way they take themselves." [88] We have seen James emphasize this dangerous tendency in his French criticism. As a Jamesian subject, Mordecai, with a great capacity for consciousness, would ultimately have strained to break out of the "aesthetic mold" that the world casts him into instead of solidifying it with a ritualistic cooperation.

Of course, the Jewish half of the book is the kind of historical or sociological venture that James would never have been tempted to try. Even in *The Bostonians* and *The Princess Casamassima* he is very careful to keep the historical scene in the background, either caricatured or reflected only in the pressures of the individual case. The strain of comedy in *The Bostonians* opens the door to social history a little wider than James's tragedy, because part of James's consistent "tragic" tone depends upon the closed door or the translucent window. But in both novels the important emphasis on the individual case and the threats to its relationship forces the background to be "aesthetically" rendered. Eliot's historicism is in the foreground because she is attracted by the "possible picturesqueness, the romance as it were—of a high moral tone." [89] We remember from James's comments on Balzac, that when temperament and tone supersede genuine moral drama the novel moves away from the James orbit. The Jamesian novelistic morality is never historically magnified or historically viewed. Nor are historical atmospheres allowed to give the consolations of "pathetic fallacy," except to the unfinished romantic temperament. Isabel must leave the ruins of Rome to face the ruins of Ralph and herself. What probably directed James's criticism of Eliot, especially the Eliot of *Daniel Deronda*, was the suggestion that, for her, the greatest moral consolations and fulfillments lay beyond the sphere of personal relationship and depended upon the sacrifice of self in the service to a larger cause, of art or social amelioration. This sacrifice demands some surrender of personal density.

Measured against James's concept of novelistic balance, Eliot leans too far too often to the side of the fixed morality of the social or Christian sphere. We have the romance of the individual case but it hardens into philosophy or softens into the picturesque; she gives us moral weight but, in the absence of a "free aesthetic life," it often remains pinned to the ground. James could see art assume many forms, but never a lifeless one, and, whereas the strong roots of Eliot's moral schemes sometimes grew in soils other than the flexible imagination, her novels could project a convincing felt life. On the other hand, unrooted imagination or sensibility in the novel quickly develops into the amoral sensuality of Baudelaire and Gautier. This temptation to amorality is even more striking when it appears in the English spirit than in the French because it is the English novel which traditionally features conscious personal adjustment to a standard morality. James turned to a poet, to Swinburne, when he sought an example of an English spirit permeated with the amoral sensibility he found abundantly on the French side. James is careful to distinguish between an artificial or imposed morality and a real or inherent one:

> We do not mean that Mr. Swinburne is not didactic, nor edifying, nor devoted to pleading the cause of virtue. We mean simply that his moral plummet does not sink at all, and that when he pretends to drop it he is simply dabbling in the relatively very shallow pool of the picturesque.[90]

When morality becomes picturesque it becomes didactic and sentimental. James is not as disturbed that Swinburne does not understand morality, "a charge to which he would be probably quite indifferent," as that "he does not at all understand immorality." [91] The James heroine learns that it is immoral *not* to be frightened by the full range and nature of Evil, for without this terror it is impossible to block what threatens to break connections. But the poetic sensibility of Swinburne is obviously not concerned with human engagement. To know the human powers of expansion, one must also know the dangers of reduction.

Of the English novelists, Dickens most obviously abuses the dramatic rendering of morality as he revels in didactic and sentimental tones. For all his variety, because he too often preferred the isolationism of melodrama to the development of relationship (this was, in fact, his *theme*), he can be only the greatest of "superficial novelists." [92] (We hardly need the light of the recent surge of sophisticated commentary on Dickens, of persistent pleas to read authors with legitimate expectations, to see how James's evaluative skill failed to handle Dickens fairly. This is especially obvious in his criticism of *Our Mutual Friend*. But this failure can be a valuable reminder that James, despite his assertion that the house of fiction has many windows, judged from his own needs and visions, and the intelligence of these requirements can be measured by the validity of so many of his perceptions and appreciations.) If Eliot could at times have used the sap of his imagination, Dickens more desperately needed the roots of Eliot's "philosophy":

> A novelist very soon has need of a little philosophy. In treating of Micawber, and Boffin, and Pickwick . . . he can . . . dispense with it, for this . . . is not serious writing. But when he comes to tell the story of a passion, a story like that of Headstone and Wray-

burn, he becomes a moralist as well as an artist. He must know *man* as well as *men,* and to know man is to be a philosopher.[93]

Without a genuine and deep moral base the novel floats unanchored on the thin waters of fancy:

> When he introduces men and women whose interest is preconceived to lie not in the poverty, the weakness, the drollery of their natures, but in their complete and unconscious subjection to ordinary and healthy human emotions, all his humor, all his fancy, will avail him nothing if, out of the fullness of his sympathy, he is unable to prosecute those generalizations in which alone consists the real greatness of a work of art.[94]

This is an important statement, for it emphasizes once more the thoroughness of James's novelistic vision which demands full projection of the author's mind. The impressiveness of that projection always depends, for James, on the quality of saturation and sympathy between author and subject. Certainly James could appreciate the uses of caricature in subject and style. His own flat characters shared in the Dickens legacy, and James must have been keenly aware of what Meredith's annoyingly tight and difficult patterns of word and gesture could, especially in a novel like *One of Our Conquerors,* do for the shift of moral concentration from society to the free individual case. But he is firm in his mistrust of that part of the novelist's mind which pampers itself with the "fantastic and the mannered" at the expense of "the splendid great moral and ethical . . . lights, and . . . big strong whiffs of manly tone and clear judgment." [95] Without a substantive anchor, the novelist is victim rather than conqueror of the metamorphic possibilities of romance. Of Meredith's *Lord Ormont* James complains:

> All elaborate predicates of exposition without the ghost of a nominative to hook themselves to; and not a difficulty met, not a figure presented, not a scene constituted—not a dim shadow condensing once either into audible or into visible reality—making you hear for an instant the tap of its feet on the earth.[96]

The "real" cable of the famous balloon of experience,[97] has been cut loose, but the cutting is detected because of the superficiality of Meredith's saturation. "Saturation" is a term which James used to describe the actual soaking of the artist in his millieu and it represents a healthy antidote to mannered superficialism. It is a process which depends for its ultimate worth upon the kind of felt life and moral imagination directing it.

4.

The concept of "saturation" fills the gap between author and subject and gives the balloon of experience its significant cargo. The weight which James missed in Dickens he found when he turned back to that novelist's French counterpart, Balzac, in whom he found a deep capacity for saturation. The author's mind, the mind that is exposed to the widest possibilities of tone, subject, and character, ought ideally to be saturated with broad life and devoted to the endless task of transmuting that material into art. In its crudest form (and James could use his favorite terms carelessly) saturation means simply documentation.

The collection of facts and objects for the novel's texture (especially the naturalistic novel) is a feverish occupation and leaves no room for wasted time (though it leads, Flaubert protested, to wasted form). Yet it is in the very leisure of time wasted that the moral application of saturation, its qualitative worth which makes collections meaningfully selective, comes about. What does *seeing* life mean for the novelist (and by extension for his characters) without *feeling* life? Zola, by simplifying the lines of his characters, by confining them "to impulses and agitations that men and women are possessed by in common," by giving us the "gregarious form . . . a picture of numbers of classes, crowds" [98] solved the problem by restricting his "knowing and showing" of life to what could be affirmed in his notes. The seeing of life alone became a theoretical ideal. But, claims James:

> It is in the *waste* . . . much rather—the waste of time, of passion, of curiosity, of contact—that true initiation resides; so that the most wonderful adventures of the artist's spirit are those, immensely quickening for his "authority," that are yet not reducible to his notes. [99]

And in a fuller commentary on Zola, James writes:

> He rests to the utmost on his documents, devours and assimilates them, makes them yield him extraordinary appearances of life. . . . We feel that he *has to* improvise for his moral and social world, the world as to which vision and opportunity must come, if they are to come at all, unhurried and unhustled—must take

their own time, helped undoubtedly more or less by blue-books, reports and interviews, by inquiries "on the spot," but never wholly replaced by such substitutes without a general disfigurement.[100]

By contrast, through sympathy and involvement, through the very waste of time these movements demand, Balzac was able, paradoxically, to save time in creation, by trusting more to instinct for the substances and characters of his saturation:

> The love, as we call it, the joy in their [his characters] communicated and exhibited movement, in their standing on their feet and going of themselves and acting out their characters, was what rendered possible the saturation I speak of; what supplied him, through the inevitable gaps of his preparation and the crevices of his prison, his long prison of labor, a short cut to the knowledge he required. It was by loving them—as the terms of his subject and the nuggets of his mind—that he knew them; it was not by knowing them that he loved.[101]

The preface to *The Princess Casamassima* tells us that James was able to find the same "short cut" for the documentation of the life of his own political waif.

By no means does saturation imply enslavement; rather its effectiveness grants freedom. The novel offers, in relation to life, the greatest opportunity and depth for the saturation process. Speaking in the broadest terms, James wrote to his brother that one chooses the form of one's saturation; [102] for James it was the novel which gave to his creative impulse at once the greatest liberation and inclusiveness. It is this potential which attracted Balzac to the novel, and James to Balzac. Balzac appreciated the novel as

> An all-inclusive form, a form without rift or leak, a tight mould, literally, into which everything relevant to a consideration of the society surrounding him—and the less relevant unfortunately, as well as the more—might be poured in a stream of increasing consistency, the underlapping subject stretched, all so formidably, to its own constituted edge and the compound appointed to reproduce, as in finest and subtlest relief, its every minutest feature, overlying and corresponding with it all round to the loss of no fraction of an inch.[103]

The reservation "and the less relevant unfortunately" warns of the danger of saturation for its own sake in novelists as voracious as

Balzac. Because ideal saturation implied, for James, sympathy, its projected weight needed moral direction. That is why metaphors for the connection between life and art often are analogous to the relationship of character to character in the novels themselves, and the loaded vessel, be it ship, balloon, or cup, is of all James's recurrent symbols, the most persistent container and preserver of deep moral conscience and involvement. The novelistic conscience, the conscience of character, and the novel itself have "nothing to fear but sailing too light." The novel "will take aboard all we bring in good faith to the dock." [104]

If the lack of dramatic saturation between life and art, author and subject was Sand's weakness and its restriction Zola's bondage, an osmotic thoroughness was Balzac's great strength. This is most clearly evidenced when there is no leakage between his great vision of incident and situation on the one hand and his rendering of dramatic character on the other:

> He is at his best when the conditions, the whole complex of subdivisible form and pressure, are virtually themselves the situation, the action and the interest, or in other words when these things exhaust themselves, as it were, in expressing the persons we are concerned with, agents and victims alike, and when by such vivified figures, whether victims or agents, they are themselves completely expressed. [105]

At these times, the weight of saturation is activated and shaped by the proper talent. But sometimes Balzac's great love of abundance forced him into an unproductive waste.

James's fiercest and, perhaps, least appealing and convincing complaints about the waste of potentially great powers of controlled saturation were reserved for the Russian novel, for Tolstoi and Dostoievsky, authors whom he viewed more often from the point of the writer's needs than that of the reader's satisfaction. The deliberate vastness of general form could not adequately direct particular character. For most readers, the energy of Dostoievsky and Tolstoi sustains their greatness, but this impression of greatness comes despite the luxury of expressive waste:

> We see how great a vice is their lack of composition, their defiance of economy and architecture, directly they are emulated and imitated; *then,* as subject of emulation, models, they quite give themselves away. There is nothing so deplorable as a work of art with

a leak in its interest; and there is no such leak of interest as through commonness of form. Its opposite, the *found* (because the sought-for) is the absolute citadel and tabernacle of interest.[106]

James saw his master economist Turgenev as the greatest projector of the "found form," the greatest enemy of waste.

In addition to an activating talent, saturation needs a subject and medium that are worth the immersion. Too thorough a saturation in an unworthy medium is dangerously binding and limiting to both writer and reader. The quality of saturation, the quality of its effect, depend upon the maturity of vision in the novelist and upon his selective taste. James talked both appreciatively and critically about the "new" English novelists, carelessly grouping Wells and Bennett with the D. H. Lawrence of *Sons and Lovers*. He was drawn to the advantage of inclusiveness that the "new" realism offered over the "old" social comedy:

> Who could pretend that Jane Austen didn't leave much more un-told than told about aspects and manners even of the confined circle in which her muse revolved? Why shouldn't it be argued against her that where her testimony complacently ends the pressure of appetite within us presumes exactly to begin? [107]

But he particularly censured Bennett for being too "saturated" in his own flat medium. Zola and his fellow naturalists had laboured under the same disadvantage. The fault, as always, goes behind the art medium to the life medium. James thought of Zola as a miser of life experience and observed, in a bit of amateur psychology, that his participation in the Dreyfus affair was "the act of a man with arrears of personal history to make up, the act of a spirit for which life, or for which at any rate freedom, had been too much postponed, treating itself at last to a luxury of experience." [108] James missed in those writers who are saturated in limiting and grim climates (Bennett, Zola) the exercise of dramatic and moral integration which transforms the ugly into the beautiful. Only through the discipline of moral direction and the responsibility of judgment could the novel's freedom be properly exploited.

Despite their different thematic concentrations, it is Conrad who seems nearest to James in the formal working out of the process of saturation. Here is a novelist fully aware of the difficulty of beauty, a "votary of the way to do a thing that shall make it undergo most doing." [109] Everyone must sense how well this describes James's own method, his own form of artistic immersion. Equally applicable to James's technique is his description of Marlow's view as "a prolonged hovering flight of the subjective over the outstretched ground of the case exposed." [110] A profitable saturation in the novelist depends ultimately upon the perfect coordination of the subjective flight and the case exposed. It is this coordination which determines impressions of intensity and complexity. When James turns again to the isolated American scene, he finds both the flight and the ground exposed, frighteningly shallow.

His many complaints about the barren ground of America for the nourishment of the novel are well known. In a famous letter to Howells, James suggests, in effect, that the novelist in America cannot depend upon the given ground for food:

> I sympathize even less with your protest against the idea that it takes an old civilization to set a novelist in motion—a proposition that seems to me so true as to be a truism. It is on manners, customs, usages, habits, forms, upon all these things matured and established, that a novelist lives—they are the very stuff his work is made of; and in saying that in the absence of those "dreary and worn-out paraphernalia" which I enumerate as being wanting in American society, "we have simply the whole of human life left," you beg (to my sense) the question. I should say we had just so much of it as these same "paraphernalia" represent, and I think they represent an enormous quantity of it. I shall feel refuted only when we have produced . . . a gentleman who strikes me as a novelist—as belonging to the company of Balzac and Thackeray.[111]

But it was not the American ground so much as the American flight that James deplored. A graver problem than the poverty of the American soil is the poverty of the American imagination. Howells is really unwilling to extend himself, his characters, to their fullest moral possibilities. Despite his adequate performances, his lack of artistic courage results in a lack of intensity. James writes in 1871 to Charles Eliot Norton:

> Looking about for myself, I conclude that the face of nature and civilization in this our country is to a certain point a very sufficient literary field. But it will yield its secrets only to a really *grasping* imagination. This I think Howells lacks.[112]

And twenty years later, even while praising *A Hazard of New Fortunes,* James reminds Howells himself that "there's a whole quarter of the heaven upon which, in the matter of composition, you seem consciously . . . to have turned your back." [113] The face of American nature and civilization, if only we do not turn our back on it, might, even if occasionally by negative reaction, give us materials adequate to make a moral and directed saturation worth while. Echoing the intensity of Roderick Hudson, James asserts:

> Civilization with us is monotonous, and in the way of contrasts, of salient points, of chiaroscuro, we have to take what we can get. We have to look for these things in fields where a less devoted glance would see little more than an arid blank, and, at the last, we manage to find them. All this refines and sharpens our perceptions, makes us in a literary way, on our own scale, very delicate, and stimulates greatly our sense of proportion and form. [114]

The American writer has to force himself in a democratized climate to a closer responsibility for the novel's potential. He certainly has manipulative freedom if he wants it, a freedom which, opened up by a lack of tradition, can be an advantage as well as a stumbling block. The way in which we preserve the advantage in the face of America's obvious toughness for the novelist is, of course, the major concern of James for his characters. As Marius Bewley puts it:

> James's fictions are the record of men and women bleakly deprived through their Puritan, democratic, and American traditions of much that constitutes life for the European artist, searching for means to satisfy their spiritual and emotional needs without sacrificing what good they already possess and which Europe cannot provide. [115]

The novelist must be more selective, more demanding, and this increase in moral intensity is asked not only of the new novelist but of his new reader as well. In one of those fervent pleas for the future of the novel which are trademarks of his critical integrity and energy, James says of "democratic" fiction:

> Our contention is exactly that, in spite of all vain aspects, it does yet present an interest, and that here and there seem written on it likelihoods of its presenting still more—always on condition of its consenting to that more intimate education which is precisely what democratized movements look most askance at. It strikes us as not too much to say that our actual view of the practice of fiction gives us as just a measure as could be desired of the general, the incurable democratic suspicion of the selective and comparative prin-

ciples in almost any application, and the tendency therewith to regard, and above all to treat, one manner of book, like one manner of person, as, if not absolutely as good as another, yet good enough for any democratic use.[116]

There is no necessary despair for the American novelist and his reader. The only ground that counts at last is the artist's own unique sensibility. His vision is his soil: "The quality and capacity of that soil, its ability to 'grow' with due freshness and straightness any vision of life, represents, strongly or weakly, the projected morality." [117] It is from the soil of this felt life that "intimate education" grows.

⊷§ III *The Burden of the Novel:*
Relationship as Morality

If a novel reveals true and vivid relationships, it is a moral work, no matter what the relationships may consist in. If the novelist *honours* the relationship in itself, it will be a great novel.[1]

D. H. Lawrence

The plea James addressed to both novelist and reader to undergo "intimate education," to face the difficulties and discomforts of honest and deep exploration, becomes for all writers who place at the center of the novel's form and meaning the concept that morality is shaped by individual personal relationship, a plea to educate for intimacy. D. H. Lawrence, like James, sees in the "collective" psychology of democracy a threat to the love of the individual case. James claims that democracy cannot read, Lawrence that democracy cannot love,[2] but they are essentially concerned about the same dangers. For all his obvious differences from James, Lawrence is closer to him on this general ground than is Conrad, whom many see as the natural disciple of James. They seem to be in strong accord when they speak of the necessity for fullness of felt life and freedom behind the novel. They agree basically that "morality in the novel is the trembling instability of the balance"[3] if we recognize that balance as the formation of dynamic relationships.

Though James's moral momentum comes from the tight interrelationship of his characters while Lawrence's more often gallops beyond this out to the larger impersonal universe, positive relational possibilities form the basic teleology of both authors. Both reject the romance of magic, but James was attracted to the humbler Cinderella-Miranda pattern of discovery and turned toward the intense domestic journey,[4] whereas Lawrence was involved with the larger Odyssey myth, the periodic circlings out to the wider universe from the domestic hearth and back again.[5] They are together when they insist:

Now here we see the beauty and the great value of the novel. Philosophy, religion, science, they are all of them busy nailing things down, to get a stable equilibrium. Religion, with its nailed-down One God, who says *Thou shalt, Thou shan't,* and hammers home every time; philosophy, with its fixed ideas; science with its "laws": they, all of them, all the time, want to nail us on to some tree or other.

But the novel, no. The novel is the highest example of subtle inter-relatedness that man has discovered. Everything is true in its own time, place, circumstance. If you try to nail anything down, in the novel, either it kills the novel, or the novel gets up and walks away with the nail.

Morality in the novel is the trembling instability of the balance. When the novelist puts his thumb in the scale, to pull down the balance to his own predilection, that is immorality. . . . The novel is a perfect medium for revealing to us the changing rainbow of our living relationships. The novel can help us to live, as nothing else can: no didactic Scripture, anyhow. If the novelist keeps his thumb out of the pan.[6]

Conrad, despite his role as "votary of the way to do a thing that shall make it undergo most doing," can be accused of trying to nail the novel down. The renunciations in James (though James's endings are prepared through steady development of a single center of consciousness) are closer to the frustrations in Lawrence (whose endings tend rather to expand outward and away from the single center of consciousness) than they are to the ironic retreats in Conrad, so jarring in a novel like *Chance.* James and Lawrence are always going toward relationship, and renunciation and frustration are symptoms of vitality, while Conrad, like Captain Anthony, fearfully approaches and then retreats from relational exploration in the paradoxically didactic and dark desire for isolation.

Just how often Lawrence's own novels walk away with the nail is another matter. But in a novel like *The Rainbow,* in which relationship as morality *is* the lyrical structure of the work, Lawrence avoids the temptation to nail down by assuming the metamorphic risks; the diffused centers of *The Rainbow* clearly leave the novel open. While James's single growing center of consciousness in the second part of *The Golden Bowl* seems to culminate in a closed ending, his "fairy tale" conclusion is only a very tenuous and temporary closing of the circle. Both *The Rainbow* and *The Golden Bowl* suggest the complexity, not the complacency, of a marital future. (This refusal to seal union artificially is perhaps what makes James complain of Jane Austen that "where her testimony complacently ends the pressure of appetite within us presumes exactly to begin.") [7] Odysseus' ship and Cinderella's carriage travel concentrically around the meanings of marriage, and their moral burdens are determined by the evolution of relationships within the vehicles. This free movement of relatedness, which leads us to open ends, is essentially dynamic and morally optimistic despite a shared penchant for frustration and renunciation. Lawrence could never forgive Conrad "for being so sad and for giving in." [8] This apparent ironic "surrender" has the same effect as the naturalistic resignation that James and Lawrence deplored in Bennett, though Bennett's relationships were reduced by determination, Conrad's by chance. When, as in Conrad, true moral and relational meaning in the "absurd" and "sad" universe is dissipated by chance, method alone has the heavy burden of providing a semblance of values. James's comments on *Chance* in "The New Novel" are almost totally concerned, implicitly, with the way in which method can save a retiring and static subject. (Action in Conrad, we sense so often, is more escape than affirmation.)

James's universe is never absurd and his values are firmly communicated. The technique of rendering is not a veil of irony that dims the truth, but a way of dramatizing the truest and most dynamic morality. The radical difference of vision between James and Conrad can be readily seen by considering Conrad's often quoted statement in "A Personal Record":

> The ethical view of the universe involves us at last in so many cruel and absurd contradictions, where the last vestiges of faith, hope, charity, and even of reason itself, seem ready to perish, that I have come to suspect that the aim of creation cannot be ethical at all. I would fondly believe that its object is purely spectacular: a spectacle for awe, love, adoration, or hate, if you like, but in this view—and in this view alone—never for despair! Those visions, delicious or poignant, are a moral end in themselves. The rest is our affair—the laughter, the tears, the tenderness, the indignation, the high tranquility of a steeled heart, the detached curiosity of a subtle mind—that's our affair! And the unwearied self-forgetful attention to every phase of the living universe reflected in our consciousness may be our appointed task on this earth. A task in which fate has perhaps engaged nothing of

us except our conscience, gifted with a voice in order to bear true testimony to the visible wonder, the haunting terror, the infinite passion and the illimitable serenity; to the supreme law and the abiding mystery of the sublime spectacle.[9]

But for the Jamesian heroine, life is never a dream, and it is a spectacle only at a partial stage of growth.

Conrad's "flexible" vision must, in order to conceive novels, allow its amorality to become didactic, and his relationship to his characters is obviously affected by his view of life. He is likely to display more subjective identity, despite the "obstacle" of the middle-man narrator, than dramatic sympathy. Conrad's tendency, in this area, is more philosophical than novelistic. Like Captain Anthony, he sees only the romance of relationship, never its reality, and it is this very vision which gave him his theme. When Conrad talks about the beginnings of his novel, *Chance,* he gives the ephemeral Flora de Barral credit for its shape:

At the crucial moment of my indecision Flora de Barral passed before me, but so swiftly that I failed at first to get hold of her. Though loth to give her up I didn't see the way of pursuit clearly and was on the point of becoming discouraged when my natural liking for Captain Anthony came to my assistance. I said to myself that if that man was so determined to embrace a "wisp of mist" the best thing for me was to join him in that eminently practical and praiseworthy adventure. I simply followed Captain Anthony. Each of us was bent on capturing his own dream.[10]

It is precisely this identification of romantic vision in character and author that prevents the "wisp of mist" from becoming relational nourishment for the novel. If Captain Anthony's dream of relationship is deliberately rendered fruitless (in spite of his "stiff" victory) by the novel's mode of irony, what does the dream mean? We certainly have no trouble judging Madame Bovary's dreams. Conrad's greatest stories depend upon ironic contradictions to the romance of the dream, constant retrogression to a static front of conduct, and upon the ultimate isolation of character, but when the novelist imitates his own hero, judgments and intentions become hopelessly confused and ambiguous. Conrad's absorption is not manifest sympathy, but rather a symbiotic escape from the individual control that sympathy demands.

The difficulty of Conrad's relationship with his own characters, and the effect this has on the relationship of characters to each other in the novels themselves, might serve as a pragmatic justification for James's concern about the nature of the felt life behind the novel. The radical distance between Conrad's defensive concept of positive conduct as an almost *a priori* moral base of the novel and the James-Lawrence concept of conduct as dependent upon relationship in metamorphosis emerges clearly when Conrad applies his leading critical ideas about the connection of life and art, his vague major standards of "sincerity and genuineness" (so much more dogmatic in their masculine guise than "taste," "amiability," or "saturation"), or his favorite images of warfare to James:

> The fiercest excitements of a romance *"de cape et d'épée,"* the romance of yard-arm and boarding pike so dear to youth, whose knowledge of action (as of other things) is imperfect and limited, are matched, for the quickening of our maturer years, by the tasks set, by the difficulties presented, to the sense of truth, of necessity —before all, of conduct—of Mr. Henry James's men and women. His mankind is delightful. It is delightful in its tenacity; it refuses to own itself beaten; it will sleep on the battlefield. These warlike images come by themselves . . . since from the duality of man's nature and the competition of individuals, the life-history of the earth must in the last instance be a history of a really very relentless warfare. Neither his fellows, nor his gods, nor his passions will leave a man alone. In virtue of these allies and enemies, he holds his precarious dominion, he possesses his fleeting significance; and it is this relation in all its manifestations, great and little, superficial or profound, and this relation alone, that is commented upon, interpreted, demonstrated by the art of the novelist in the only possible way in which the task can be performed; by the independent creation of circumstance and character, achieved against all the difficulties of expression, in an imaginative effort finding its inspiration from the reality of forms and sensations.[11]

What he says is true of James's men and women and, in a sense, of Lawrence's as well, since all degrees of relationship are specified. But neither of these novelists would share Hardy's view of life as a battlefield upon which small tenacious Man struggles to achieve final definition of conduct and character as a minute part of the life history of the earth. What brings Lawrence and James close together in this instance and what separates them from Conrad is that for them individual human relationships in themselves usurp the throne of all fixed standards of conduct; the personal felt life and vision brought to the novel participate sympathetically in these relationships and submit the novel not just to the temper of irony but also to that of love. It is the individual man himself who will not give up his relatedness with fellow, god, or passion, not vice versa. While Conrad works in the passive voice, James and Lawrence work in the active.

For both Lawrence and James the following syllogistic belief was central: "If a novel reveals true and vivid relationships, it is a moral work, no matter what the relationships may consist in. If the novelist *honours* the relationship in itself, it will be a great novel." [12] Whether it develop in the Odysseus or the Miranda-Cinderella world, relationship grows out of an active love between man and man, and most significantly, between man and woman. The unpardonable sin for both James and Lawrence is deadening a circuit. Osmond's real sin is the desire to make portraits out of lives. And the sin of Skrebensky is the easy acceptance of the trivial, the immediate, the dimensionless, the unfeeling, the unrelated. Though Skrebensky's case reflects the wider picture of specific cultural disintegrations that makes him seem more a victim than a villain, his barren saturation in his role is to be judged, like Osmond's, immoral on the personal plane.

An equally deadening substitution is a satanic unconquerable will for any relationship at all. Dostoievsky, whose waste was censured by James, is condemned by Lawrence because so many of his seemingly powerful relationships are not genuine but imposed. The Dostoievsky character cannot effect a state of consistent relatedness. Dostoievsky's "mania to be infinite" which tends to Christian selflessness, on the one hand, and his passion for the "fixed will" which ends in the absolute self on the other hand, lead to the dissolution, not confirmation of relation. After all, Lawrence maintains, fallen angels do not have relationships; they seek only to return to an isolated purity.[13] For both James and Lawrence, the novel, like the life, which rejects isolation and imposition and sponsors instead free relatedness will carry the deepest meanings because it carries the deepest morality. All the rest is *"de la littérature."* Lawrence is so passionately devoted to the pure structure of relationship that he goes beyond James to the near obliteration of person:

And the relation between man and woman will change for ever, and will for ever be the new central clue to human life. It is the *relation itself* which is the quick and central clue to life, not the man, nor the woman, nor the children that result from the relationship, as a contingency.[14]

We may now begin to question the alliance of Lawrence and James. We can assume that what, in James's view, makes Lawrence "hang in the dusty rear" [15] of the "new" novelists is the apparent social and psychological determinism of *Sons and Lovers*. Actually, of course, Lawrence spins his major characters out of the circle of fate, as Kate Croy is flung out of her naturalistic beginnings, in the interests of individual responsibility. Both novelists ferry relationship beyond its societal determinants for the sake of a deeper moral drama. Both were certain that the new relationship could work as structural as well as ideological center for the novel. But the Odyssean diet contains too much universe for Cinderella to digest. Eventually, the idea of relationship obliterated personality and became in Lawrence's world more binding than the history that gave birth to a personality, too ritualistic in itself for application in the world of James. For ritual is anathema to James, the very enemy of relationship, and *The Wings of the Dove* is a tragedy of the potential of relationship reduced to sterility by ritual, of the free, rich, and innocent pressed into the service of a metaphor (the dove).

The systematized Laurentian world poised on four prime poles in the individual, reaching first to four prime poles in another individual, and then to the circuit of the universe itself [16] revolves far from the hearth of Maggie and her prince. For Lawrence:

> The ritual of the great events in the year of stars is for nations and whole peoples. To these rituals we must return: or we must evolve them to suit our needs. For the truth is, we are perishing for lack of fulfillment of our greater needs, we are cut off from the great sources of our inward nourishment and renewal sources which flow eternally in the universe.[17]

From this blanching of the individual relationship it is not too far to travel to an utter disgust with personality, a disgust which James was unable to feel, which, indeed, would have killed his whole novelistic passion that depended so much upon the dramatic individuality of his characters. In his desire for purity in relationship, Lawrence revolts against the "fingering over our own souls" and asks for "a new common life, a new complete tree of life from the roots that are within us." [18] It might seem as if Lawrence is again merely objecting to the isolationism of the Dostoievsky autonomous personality. But this disgust develops rapidly into a rejection of the novel itself:

> Philosophy interests me most now—not novels or stories. I find people ultimately boring: and you can't have fiction without

people. So fiction does not, at bottom, interest me any more. I am weary of humanity and human things. One is happy in the thoughts only that transcend humanity.[19]

The promise of relationship in the first part of *The Plumed Serpent* turns to display of ritual in the second. This is an "expansion" that never tempted James. For James, universal drama had meaning only in the soul of a Maggie.

Paradoxically, perhaps, the more deeply James mined the personal vein, the more the historical sense in his work seems to give way to the symbolic. His most fully developed novel of relationship, *The Golden Bowl,* represents the widest rhythmic expansion of competition between marital and parental influence, yet it is enacted with a central consciousness, and metaphor is never independent of personality. Though sociological critics may find interesting cultural symptoms in *The Golden Bowl,* we could hardly call it a dedicated and tendentious social commentary or a personal plea for the future in the Laurentian tradition. Even in *The Princess Casamassima,* politics is to Hyacinth, ironically, a promise of fulfillment of the personal dimension he yearns for. Despite the frequent assumption that this novel deviates from the mainstream of James's most typical work, *The Princess Casamassima* clearly works with the same pattern as the later novels: instead of the determinism of American romanticism as background we have the American projection of happiness and the sense of the "special case" which prepare the hero for his martyrdom. This romantic expectation, cherished by Hyacinth as well as his "family," cooperates with naturalistic exploitation. Hyacinth is as much a composed "dove" as Milly Theale, and his tragedy as much as hers is that of isolation from relationship. While Lawrence derides sarcastically the indomitable hope for happiness in American consciousness, James uses it as a dramatic metaphor to explain the personal rather than the cultural pattern. James's politics do not recommend; he never lets the boundaries of art dissolve for those of life. He is not apocalyptic so he depends exclusively upon particular conscious characters, upon the individual case, to carry moral weight, a dependence that became distasteful to Lawrence.

The dramatic struggle between the mother and the father, the feminine sensibility and the masculine ego, for the soul of the relational novelist, or character, is recognized by James in his *Autobiography*. It was his mother who taught James to keep his thumb out of the pan:

How can I better express what she seemed to do for her second son than by saying that even with her deepest delicacy of attention present I could still feel, while my father read, why it was that I most of all seemed to wish we might have been either much less religious or much more so? Was not the reason at bottom that I so suffered, I might almost have put it, under the impression of his style, which affected me as somehow too philosophic for life, and at the same time too living, as I made out, for thought?—since I must weirdly have opined that by so much as you were individual, which meant personal, which meant monotonous, which meant limitedly allusive and verbally repetitive, by so much you were not literary or, so to speak, *largely* figurative. My father had terms, evidently strong, but in which I presumed to feel, with a shade of irritation, a certain narrowness of exclusion as to images otherwise —and oh, since it was a question of the pen, so multitudinously— entertainable. Variety, variety—*that* sweet ideal, *that* straight contradiction of any dialectic, hummed for me all the while as a direct, if perverse and most unedified, effect of the parental concentration, with some of its consequent, though heedless, dissociations. I heard it, felt it, saw it, both shamefully enjoyed and shamefully denied it as form, though as form only; and I owed thus supremely to my mother that I could, in whatever obscure levity, muddle out some sense of my own preoccupation under the singular softness of the connection that she kept for me, by the outward graces, with that other and truly much intenser which I was so little framed to share.[20]

Both James and Lawrence felt the danger, strongly enunciated in Lawrence's criticism of Dostoievsky, of the imposition of fixed and self-sealing personality in the novel, but Lawrence reacted by sublimating character to its relationship, while James turned to the particular character to expose itself to new relationship. Ultimately, Lawrence's masculine sensibility preferred relationship as ritual, while James's primarily feminine sensibility rendered relationship dramatic. James at least implicitly assumed that the masculine sensibility of the novelist is essentially religious or philosophical; the feminine sensibility is rather social. George Eliot had, in James's view, harbored a competition between the two sensibilities, and had succeeded at her best in bringing them richly together. James himself, as biographical critics like Quentin Anderson would probably maintain, controlled his dominant feminine strain by strong infusions of the masculine, but the preference between the two sensibilities is forcefully expressed in another page of James's *Autobiography:*

Feeling myself "after" persons so much more than after anything else—to recur to that side of my earliest and most constant consciousness which might have been judged most deplorable—I take it that I found the sphere of our more nobly suppositious habitation too imperceptibly peopled; where as the religious life of every other family that could boast of any such . . . affected my fancy as with a social and material crowdedness. . . . All of which, at the same time . . . I allow myself to add, didn't mitigate the simple fact of my felt—my indeed so luxuriously permitted—detachment of sensibility from everything, everything, that is, in the way of great relations, as to which our father's emphasis was richest. *There* was the dim dissociation, there my comparative poverty, or call it even frivolity, of instinct: I gaped imaginatively, as it were, to such a different set of relations. I couldn't have framed stories that would have succeeded in involving the least of the relations that seemed most present to *him;* while those most present to myself, that is more complementary to whatever it was I thought of as humanly most interesting, attaching, inviting, were the ones his schemes of importance seemed virtually to do without.[21]

James recognizes, through a touching paradox, the loss that this vision represents for the potential novelist:

None the less, however, I remember it as savouring of loss to me —which is my present point—that our so thoroughly informal scene of susceptibility seemed to result from a positive excess of familiarity, in his earlier past, with such types of the shepherd and the flock, to say nothing of such forms of the pasture, as might have met in some degree my appetite for the illustrational.[22]

The freeing of religion from the particular minister and congregation was to the mind of the novelist an enslavement. Again and again the universal meanings of relationship for James had to be dramatically particularized in his characters.

Aware of the advantages which the feminine sensibility brought to his own development, James was anxious to trace its positive contributions to the English novel at large. If the feminine sensibility has at times made the English novel prudish or conventional it has also given it, according to James, the emphasis of personal relationship:

It is the ladies in a word who have lately done most to remind us of man's relations with himself, that is with woman. His relations with the pistol, the pirate, the police, the wild and the tame beast —are not these prevailingly what the gentlemen have given us? [23]

The true feminine sensibility is interested in character, not figures. When it is perverted by authors, James warns:

There is surely no principle of fictitious composition so true as this,—that an author's paramount charge is the cure of souls, to the subjection, and if need be to the exclusion, of the picturesque. Let him look to his characters: his figures will take care of themselves.[24]

Yielding to the temptation of the picturesque means putting the thumb in the scale, and it is the feminine sensibility which teaches us to keep our thumbs out of the pan. If Lawrence dissolves character in relationship, the practitioners of the picturesque, we remember, block relationship before it starts. At its best, the genuine feminine sensibility can give us two things in the novel: personal relationship as a moral center and the freedom that developing character demands from the bondage of society, ideology, and the picturesque. That is why James is particularly severe on abuses of feminine sensibility. Of Miss Prescott's characters he exclaims: "Good heavens, Madam! . . . let the poor things speak for themselves. What? Are you afraid they can't stand alone?" [25] It is only with this apparent granting of autonomy to character that the feminine sensibility can, painfully, carefully, and meaningfully bring together personal relationship and morality, until each defines itself in terms of the other.

A distinctive revelation which emerges from an integrated reading of James's literary criticism and the novels themselves is the similarity in preparation for life of both the novelist and his characters. Because the judgments of novelist and character are exposed to the same dangers, we can expect that the dialectic of terms which defined novelistic visions, naturalistic vs. romantic, picturesque or aesthetic vs. realistic or moral, would be found again in the visions of the characters themselves. The obsessive metaphors cross the boundaries with ease and frequency. Maupassant's "perfectly dead wall" looms up in front of Isabel (who is deprived of relational fulfillment):

She had taken all the first steps in the purest confidence, and then she had suddenly found the infinite vista of a multiplied life to be a dark, narrow alley with a dead wall at the end.[26]

We think of the many references in James's criticism to the soil of the artist's subject when the Baroness of *The Europeans* says:

"Her irritation came, at bottom, from the sense, which, always present, had, suddenly grown acute, that the social soil on this big, vague continent was somehow not adapted for growing those plants whose fragrance she especially inclined to inhale. . . ." [27]

And we appreciate the irony of offensive authorship when Isabel reflects, after her recognition of deception, that Osmond wanted her for "a pretty piece of property." [28] She interprets his intention like this: "He would rake the soil gently and water the flowers." This reference, if we remember James's critical doctrines, goes beyond its function in the general garden imagery of the novel itself. Also, James's favorite metaphor of "launching" is scattered throughout both fiction and criticism, and, with allowances for the different functions of each discipline, the vessels sail in the same direction. James always delighted in granting his great heroines more and more freedom and power to compose their own lives, and the adjustment of their vision in image no less than action meant the fulfillment of the novel's structure.

James's use of the two sensibilities is nowhere as systematized a dialectic as Lawrence's, and his associations are decidedly different. Yet his major novels implicitly dramatize the contest he explicitly pictures in his *Autobiography*. The feminine is not to be equated with the passive, the masculine with the active, since the most dynamic influence is inevitably feminine. This is probably one reason he preferred heroines. Both sensibilities are lodged, of course, in each of the sexes. In a novel of the middle period, *What Maisie Knew,* James shows us the childhood of a feminine sensibility that works through relational pains and possibilities. It is the same symbolic childhood that Isabel Archer had to grow through and that Milly Theale and Maggie Verver would inherit from her:

> To live with all intensity and perplexity and felicity in its terribly mixed little world would thus be the part of my interesting small mortal; bringing people together who would be at least more correctly separate; keeping people separate who would be at least more correctly together; flourishing, to a degree, at the cost of many conventions and proprieties, even decencies, really keeping the torch of virtue alive in an air tending infinitely to smother it; really in short making confusion worse confounded by drawing some stray fragrance of an ideal across the scent of selfishness, by sowing on barren strands, through the mere fact of presence, the seed of the moral life.[29]

The moral sense which flourishes so prematurely in Maisie interfuses her sense of true relationship. (The corruption in terms of her own desire for manipulation at the end of the novel is a regular part of the growth process in the Jamesian heroine, though it is not always so explicitly sketched.) The immorality which threatens to smother Maisie's "torch of virtue" is not principally societal but personal. It inheres not so much in the physical and social substitution of one set of relationships for another, as in the fact that by this substitution there has been no gain in depth or honesty. The meshing of the moral and relational strands through the agency of an active feminine sensibility in the major James novels is especially apparent when societal standards of moral conduct are contradicted by personal standards and when truth to the personal relationship establishes a finer morality than convention has to offer. Why do we feel so much strength in and sympathy for perpetrators of the unpardonable sin, Kate Croy, Charlotte Stant, and even, at times, Madame Merle? It is because, in each case, there is at the center of a profoundly selfish behaviour (whether initiated by an over-dominant masculine will or a misdirected feminine sensibility) the desire to be true to a relationship of long duration, a desire that lifts Madame Merle above Osmond.[30] Charlotte's marriage to Adam Verver is not so much a punishment for moral misconduct as it is a way of correcting the false expectation that relationship could thrive on secret afternoons and incidents. It is obviously not the social morality of Mrs. Lowder which thwarts Kate's union, but the establishment of a finer relationship than Kate has to offer.

It is the masculine will that raises the status of relationship to a religious or romantic ritual, but it is the feminine sensibility that keeps relationship alive by disturbing ritual, by submitting it to the tests of change. It is the masculine idea of marriage as ritual and high moral purpose which helps lead Isabel back to Osmond, but the hope for life over death depends upon the feminine determination to break through the portrait of life and to create new circuits of relatedness. It is this flexibility which makes of Chad Newsome's and Mme de Vionnet's social adultery personally "a virtuous attachment" while it is in Strether's as yet uninitiated and social eyes still a disconcerting idea.

One measure of the masculine will is the resistance it offers to or arouses in personal attachments. (Mrs. Newsome and Caspar Goodwood are flat embodiments of the dogmatism of the masculine will.) Though Strether gains a working feminine sensibility perhaps too late in life to be saved by it, he is granted its internal influence, and he finds before him a living example of the possible moral extensions of true relationship. (It is significant, and not at all paradoxical, that the world of Woollett, which Strether eventually turns his back on, is called a "society of women." [31] One can make obvious analogies to the "masculinity" of the atmosphere in *The Bostonians*.) It is through Strether's *new* sense of the attachment that its worth becomes more than it actually is. His own feminine sensibility has broken through the canvas.

The Ambassadors is essentially an intensive revaluation of morality and emphasizes a shifting of ethical norm from the base of provincial isolationism to that of relational freedom. Little Bilham's reference to the union of Chad and Mme de Vionnet as "a virtuous attachment" is, of course, not really a lie, and the making of a profound truth out of a "technical" lie is the climax of the book (pp. 112-113; p. 359). It is ironically Mme de Vionnet who sows on barren strands the seed of moral life. It is in her boat that Strether wants to be launched (p. 233).

Though James became more and more luxuriantly profuse in his water imagery that equated engagement in life with the proper launching to sea, nowhere does he so finely bring together the literal and the figurative strands to reflect the thematic climax as in *The Ambassadors*. Wandering in the country, before his climactic encounter with Chad and Mme de Vionnet in the boat, Strether reflects that "though he had been alone all day, he had never yet struck himself as so engaged with others, so in midstream of his drama" (p. 331). As yet he has only the idea of relationship in his mind, the picture of it, the romance of it. (Early in the novel, Strether, still under the influence of Woollett, was concerned with the *appearance* of his own morality: "Was he to renounce all amusement for the sweet sake of that authority? And *would* such renunciation give him for Chad a moral glamour?" [p. 57]) He is about to witness (not, alas, experience) the reality of it. Much earlier Strether had realized of Mme de Vionnet that "by a turn of the hand she had somehow made their encounter a relation" (p. 153). The possibility of relationship, which Strether finally discerns as the center of life, has so changed his values that he sees himself comically defensive in the face of Chad's casual faith. Chad mentions to Strether that it is "good relations" which keep him in Paris. And Strether asks, initiating a lively dialectic:

"And what *are* your good relations?"
"That's exactly what you'll make out if you'll only go, as I'm supplicating you, to see her." . . . Again Strether had faltered, but

it was brief. It was all very well, but there was nothing now he
wouldn't risk.

"Excuse me, but I must really—as I began by telling you—know
where I am. Is she bad?"

"Bad?" Chad echoed it, but without shock. "Is that what's implied?"

"When relations are good?" Strether felt a little silly. . . . (p. 147)

The entire novel is filled with play, to the point of punning, upon
the word "relation," and both the verbal and emotional movements
of the novel depend upon the passage from encounter to relation.
As in *The Portrait* and all the late novels, the basic terms of Jamesian
morality, "good," "virtuous," "innocent," are tested and redefined.
The sub-plot of Waymarsh and his daily affairs is a measure of the
possible distance between shallow and deep relationship, shallow and
deep morality.

The mind of Strether expands from a pictured romance of relationship to the sense of its dynamic reality, an expansion that all of
James's major heroines must also endure. Isabel for a while plays
only with the pictures and possibilities of alliance. At the end of her
novel she turns away from Goodwood to Osmond, only partly because of her promise to Pansy (the hope of her life relived) and
only partly because promise is itself the ritual of marriage. We feel
a greater motivation to be her compulsive recognition that there has
been a tragic and uncalculated failure of relationship that must be
made good. Although ritual enslaves it can also be a challenge to
those who see clearly. Goodwood's offered temptation, a new romance
of life, is the death she has just come from. It is the same old
trap she had set for herself. Even more important is Isabel's realization that the privilege of loving was greater than the benefits
from being loved. When Goodwood asks: "Why should you go back
—why should you go through that ghastly form?" Isabel answers:
"To get away from *you!*" [32] James adds: "But this expressed only
a little of what she felt. The rest was that she had never been loved
before." It is an overwhelming feeling which weakens her will and
understanding with sexual "threats." But the love of Warburton, the
devotion of Ralph could not turn her away from an active direction.
She is impelled by the old heroism of compositional determination
in the face of chaos and collapse. Her sketch will be, like Ralph's, a
reduced one (for she too is suffering from sickness), but she sends

us back to the beginning of the novel where James had observed of Ralph:

> If he was consideringly disposed, something told him, here was occupation enough for a succession of days. It may be added, in summary fashion, that the imagination of loving—as distingushed from that of being loved—had still a place in his reduced sketch. (I, 54) [33]

In keeping with the *Paradise Lost* imagery permeating the last part of *The Portrait,* the long summer afternoon becomes a long day's dying, but out of this hell Isabel must somehow construct a paradise within. Though she envies Ralph his real dying, she recognizes that "life would be her business for a long time to come" (II, 392). Death would be a romantic solution, or dissolution. The over-lyrical style of her temptation (II, 391) reminds us of this. Like the despairing Adam viewing the pageant of the future, Isabel sees, just before Goodwood's kiss, the world as large, but not as much this time with possibility, as with pain. When it takes the form of "a mighty sea, where she floated in fathomless waters" (II, 435), we are reminded once more of James's famous condolence letter to Grace Norton in which he pits the density of individual consciousness against the temptation to melt into the universe. No true James heroine is allowed to stagnate on the bench of desolation in the gardens of the world or to float aimlessly in a hermetic ark. And like Eve, the original victim of the romantic vision, Isabel still carries the dream of Eden within her as her idea of marriage. She will start now with the hollow "observance of a magnificent form" (II, 356). Like Pascal's novitiate seeker of faith, she will bend her knees and bow her head and perhaps then faith will follow. She can now use the aesthetic idea of marriage instead of allowing it to use her, and work to infuse it with moral life.[34] As a heroine of the middle period, Isabel does not yet have the power over her fate that James grants to Maggie, and we might question whether Isabel's return is not still the romantic substitution of stubborn pride for insight, whether it is not, in fact, an ironic fulfillment of romantic determinism. Still, we can grant it the superior nobility that comes from the impression that a conscious Isabel is feeling the power of choice. James's irony is never that ungenerous to those he loves.

Isabel is as guilty for the failure of her marriage, in a sense as Osmond, for her penchant for the picturesque had blocked her vision of the real. What unites her to Osmond is not the guilt between victimizer and victim, nor the devotion of martyred nobility to what martyrs it, but rather the honor between thieves. Osmond was able to use her, to court her in terms of the picturesque, and in terms of a false romance, only because she was willing to see relationship romantically and picturesquely instead of realistically. In James, the immorality of the picturesque vision matches the immorality of the romantic vision when it is isolated from the real. This is how Isabel had seen Osmond:

> A certain combination of features had touched her, and in them she had seen the most striking of figures. That he was poor and lonely and yet that somehow he was noble—that was what had interested her and seemed to give her her opportunity. There had been an indefinable beauty about him—in his situation, in his mind, in his face. . . . He was like a sceptical voyager strolling on the beach while he waited for the tide, looking seaward yet not putting to sea. It was in all this she had found her occasion. She would launch his boat for him; she would be his providence. . . . (II, 192)

If Isabel had been cognizant of the patterns of James's imagery she might have seen through the romance of her vision, as so many of her modern critics have done. Her picture of marriage is as romantic as the traditional vision of the saint who will reform the sinner. It is this penchant, then, that feeds Osmond's opportunism, and it is no accident (any more than Rodolphe's studied rhetoric in *Madame Bovary*) that he uses the romantic and picturesque images calculated most to appeal to Isabel:

> "My dear girl, I can't tell you how life seems to stretch there before us—what a long summer afternoon awaits us. It's the latter half of an Italian day—with a golden haze, and the shadows just lengthening, and that divine delicacy in the light, the air, the landscape, which I have loved all my life and which you love to-day." (II, 81)

In a way, Osmond's deception, in comparison to Isabel's is simple; his vision of life is consistently, even if perversely, sincere. He practices a rhetoric of honesty (I, 383). Isabel herself realizes in the climactic moment of her decision to go to Ralph that Osmond "in his wish to preserve appearances . . . was after all sincere" (II, 357). It is simply that his vision of life always underrates, is even at its deepest naturalistic; his relations are either to things, or to people as things, and this position complements Isabel's romantic notions.

How dangerously close Isabel's original romantic vision is in effect to Osmond's naturalistic vision is shown by her desire to make art out of Pansy's life in much the same way that Osmond wants to keep Isabel a portrait. She sees Pansy as a blank page that begs for sketching (II, 26). Osmond had already accused her of wanting to make a work of art out of her own life (II, 15). There are plenty of others who are willing to do this for her, even the best, Ralph Touchett. This is perhaps Isabel's gravest error, and a typically romantic one, that she saw herself as Osmond (and Ralph) wanted her to, as a portrait.

Though gardens in James hold the promise of Edens revisited, they hold the serpent of romantic temptation as well. We remember that Isabel had, after all, fallen in love with the portrait of Osmond:

> the image of a quiet, clever, sensitive, distinguished man, strolling on a moss-grown terrace above the sweet Val d'Arno and holding by the hand a little girl whose bell-like clearness gave a new grace to childhood. The picture had no flourishes, but she liked its lowness of tone and the atmosphere of summer twilight that pervaded it. It spoke of the kind of personal issue that touched her most nearly; of the choice between objects, subjects, contacts—what might she call them?—of a thin and those of a rich association; of a lonely, studious life in a lovely land; of an old sorrow that sometimes ached today; of a feeling of pride that was perhaps exaggerated, but that had an element of nobleness; of a care for beauty and perfection so natural and so cultivated together that the career appeared to stretch beneath it in the disposed vistas and with the ranges of steps and terraces and fountains of a formal Italian garden—allowing only for arid places freshened by the natural dews of a quaint half-anxious, half-helpless fatherhood. (I, 399-400)

This same temptation of "quaint half-anxious, half-helpless fatherhood" later becomes the garden romance which Maggie must resist. *The Portrait* is filled with confrontation between the world of the picturesque-romantic (the world of roles) and the world of real relationship (the world of subjects).

We have said that James liked to grant his heroines compositional powers in the later novels. With Isabel, the youngest of the great heroines, we see most clearly the beginning stages of this process. The heroine must first be composed romantically by herself, then opportunistically by others, until finally she herself earns the rights of mature authorship. James's heroines persistently conceive of themselves, during their early stages of only partial vision, as heroines of novels, a self-image which complements, of course, the portrait and which works against development. This is a vision which Emma Bovary never outgrows. This tendency is most fully exploited in *The Sacred Fount,* but the premarital Isabel herself lives in the world of the romantic novel.

She had early seen England and Gardencourt as pictures of romance and says of Warburton (though James allows her the tone of humorous exaggeration): "Oh, I hoped there would be a lord; it's just like a novel!" (I, 18). In an early chat with Mr. Touchett, who, like Adam Verver, seems "a placid, homely household god" (I, 74), Isabel shows how close fiction is to reality in her young mind. She says of the English men in regard to American girls: "I don't believe they're very nice to girls; they're not nice to them in the novels." And Mr. Touchett answers knowingly: "I don't know about the novels . . . I believe the novels have a great deal of ability, but I don't suppose they're very accurate" (I, 76-77). When Henrietta expresses her concern about Isabel's aimless freedom and asks her about her goal, Isabel's answer is dangerously close to Emma Bovary's: "I haven't the least idea, and I find it very pleasant not to know. A swift carriage, of a dark night, rattling with four horses over roads that one can't see—that's my idea of happiness." And Henrietta replies significantly: "Mr. Goodwood certainly didn't teach you to say such things as that—like the heroine of an immoral novel" (I, 235). Henrietta shares with Isabel the American penchants for theory over practice (perhaps a necessary defensive measure), for allegorizing personality, for judging quickly and expressing honestly, and for maintaining the illusion of perfect freedom and full potentiality; and she shares the affliction of "meagre knowledge" combined with "inflated ideals" (I, 69). But because she is not slated for expansion of "spirit in a waste of shame," she might be the one to wonder with Voyt: "And what is the honest lady doing on that side of the town?"

Literary allusion itself in *The Portrait,* principally to *Paradise Lost* and *The Tempest,* provides the ironic reference necessary for the exposure of romantic vision. Ralph and Henrietta, forced backstage by death and comedy and unable to share Isabel's scenes of engagement, readily and sportively cast themselves in the drama of her soul.

The Tempest gives them the theme of possibility for romance in the real world and also exaggerates the metamorphoses of life (we remember James's attraction to the Miranda-Cinderella stories). Ralph claims that he cannot after all help Isabel in life, because he is merely Caliban, not Prospero, and Henrietta answers: "You were Prospero enough to make her what she has become. You've acted on Isabel Archer since she came here, Mr. Touchett" (I, 169).

But Ralph, for all his desire to shape the life he is losing to Osmond, belongs neither to the sphere of magic nor of the romantic novel. He cannot put the world to sleep; he cannot protect Isabel-Miranda from the disappointments of the brave new world she sees through her partial and romantic vision. On the contrary, it is he who gives her the terrible chance to test her virtue. Henrietta is a clumsy Ariel, helpless without Prospero's magic, and James would always decline the part of Prospero. Ralph, the self-styled Caliban, who knows he must renounce love for death, is pained by the waking state, and after his enormous disappointment in Isabel's marriage he can only cry to dream again. The seemingly magic metamorphoses in James's novels are effected by the real suffering and real learning in his characters, and just as he must keep his thumb out of the pan, so must his potential fictional saviours. So concerned is James that Isabel be free to face the ultimate risks of the metamorphic state that he twists Prospero's tools of magic into ironic use, and Ralph's staff and book give Isabel money rather than love, exposing her, not to the brave new world, but to the cold old one. Being only human, Ralph cannot wait until his Miranda is ready for the real world. Significantly, when Isabel is ready to revise her idea of freedom, to recognize its responsibilities, she speaks in the language of James's prefaces:

> If ever a girl was a free agent, she had been. A girl in love was doubtless not a free agent; but the sole source of her mistake had been within herself. There had been no plot, no snare. (II, 160).

As the novel draws to a close, she will take the pen from the hands of Ralph, Goodwood, Osmond, Henrietta, Warburton, from all who asked: "What have you done with your life?" She will no longer see through literature. In the face of Ralph's death, "she had never been less interested in literature" (II, 424).

Like Milly Theale, Isabel is launched into this novel a virtual orphan, a state ideally suited for relational exploration, and ultimately she seeks the engagement of familial acceptance and responsibility. When she turns in the end to the task of making marriage more than role and ritual, she will instinctively go to Pansy to make the ritual of her promise mean more than the romantic role of parenthood, the role that has been part of Osmond's attraction for her. She hopes for real parenthood, not stepmotherdom, even if she can barely hope for real wifedom. Her capacity for engagement makes it painful for her to persist in false parental and marital roles as does Mrs. Touchett, who maintains only ritual without relationship, only conduct without capacity.

One might repeat without flippancy, that in James, relationship begins at home. This is certainly a truth that Isabel passes on to Maggie. Adoption can anchor true relationship (as that of Isabel to Ralph and Mr. Touchett, or that of Isabel to Pansy) or it can remain frozen in social propriety (as does Kate's adoption by Mrs. Lowder). (Because Kate's own "adoption" of Milly is far more crassly directed than Mrs. Lowder's of Kate, it is no wonder that it is the adopted who must give of self to the adopter, even posthumously.) Isabel and Maggie, on the other hand, have a chance to give living gifts of engagement to their adoptees, and part of the righting of the balance in *The Golden Bowl* depends upon Charlotte's becoming the adopted instead of the adopter in connection with Maggie, upon her accepting the father whose withdrawal converts his child to wife.

Particularly in James's late novels the isolating romantic vision had always to be chastened by the relating realistic vision within the center of consciousness. Maggie's Prince had finally to be seen as a subject before he could be an agent and term of relationship. The text of *The Ivory Tower* in its fragmented state clearly reveals that this concern was as central to the formation of the novel as the characters themselves. When Horton Vint protests the romantic naïveté behind his appointment to personal and financial responsibility by Gray Fiedler, an appointment which seems to open more paths of opportunism than he ever dreamed of, he calls Gray "insanely romantic." Gray defends himself by claiming: "I'm never so reasonable, so deliberate, so lucid and so capable— . . . as when I'm most romantic." [35] He goes on to assert that his trust in Vint implies a relation, not a prejudice, because a relation "is exactly a *fact* of reciprocity" (p. 234). He refuses "not to believe tremendous things of any subject of a relation of mine." The words sound impressively fine, but it is time for the romantic vision to be anchored, and Vint,

who is as flattened by cynicism as Gray is by idealism, nevertheless
has over Gray the advantage of understanding the basis of real relationship, even if he can not effect it. He asks: "Any subject?" and
then submits:

> "That condition . . . will cut down not a little your general possi-
> bilities of relation. . . . In this country one's a figure . . . on easy
> terms; and if I correspond to your idea of the phenomenon you'll
> have much to do—I won't say for my simple self, but for the com-
> fort of your mind—to make your fond imagination fit the funny
> facts." [36]

That Gray has spent an uprooted youth away from this reductive
cynicism is a fact that unites him with the American heroines of
the late James novels whose romantic vision sees relationship only
as figure. This vision is a particularly American heritage, but it is
always a heritage that saves while it condemns, for if the initial seeing of reality as larger than life plunges characters into painful
purgatories of experience, it also allows them to emerge after exposure
to the real world with a roundness that is denied the "naturalistic"
continental souls. One might conjecture that this phenomenon is an
outcome of the famous "splits" that critics from de Tocqueville to
Santayana have spotted in American culture. Perhaps Isabel, Milly,
and Maggie, in their early isolating romantic vision, are victims of
Santayana's transcendental fallacy which separates belief from tradition by chaining it to the unique creative self. Then, conscious of the
isolation from real relationship inherent in the strain of romance in
the American novel, James, we might contend, exposes the American
character to Europe not only for cultural or merely experiential education to heal the split between ways and opinions, but more crucially
as a necessary prospecting for the gold of rounded relationship.
The international exchange has more metaphorical than actual importance. Gold is possible only when the romantic vision is first
inherited and then corrected. This implies the destruction of the
theatrical consciousness of role that keeps the heroine from the real
engagement.

James might have well used Fyodor Pavlovitch Karamazov's mocking recognition of his own passion for the romantic role, for the picturesque, as an object lesson to his heroines. In themselves the aesthetic attractions of role and romance may seem pleasantly harmless,
but when they enter into the center of life and subsume judgment

and conduct, they invite mortal danger. When Dostoievsky's Karamazov admits that all his life he had been "taking offence on aesthetic
grounds," [37] he condemns himself to isolation. Osmond's terrible
isolation comes from his preference for "superior material" over
"superior morality" (II, 144).

When one is absorbed in creating role instead of relationship, one
is a victim of the romantic vision. The essential drives of the romantic hero in the naturalistic world, and Don Quixote is a perfect test
case, are the desire to be used and the horror of using. To be used
means that one, in a sense, belongs, and this is a tempting security
for the American heroine. When Isabel sees in Goodwood the same
romantic vision of personality which she has attempted to purge in
herself, she resists, for she realizes that with him she herself would
be forced into the role of user.

One of the comforts of the romantic vision is that by oversimplifying it makes life easier. This is true not only in the definition of individuals, but in the national and international case, too. We have seen
what Isabel's unchastened imagination made of England. Her first
exclamations in Gardencourt promise future tragedy; but while romanticism is directed to a history it cannot hurt, it affords an almost
comic relief. James is too sensitive about the cultural insecurity he
feels for his native land to take such irresponsibility lightly. The
American consciousness as a whole, he says, is obsessed with the creation of a romantic role it can come to terms with:

> The novelists improvise, with the aid of historians, a romantic
> local past of costume and compliment and swordplay and gallantry
> and passion; the dramatists build up, of a thousand pieces, the airy
> fiction that the life of the people in the world among whom the
> elements of clash and contrast are simplest and most superfi-
> cial abounds in the subjects and situations and effects of the
> theatre. . . .[38]

Superficial clash and contrast compete with the agony of real relationship that the feminine sensibility brings to the pirate world.

Nowhere in James is the tragedy of a relationship frozen by romantic and naturalistic visions so poignantly treated as in *The Wings
of the Dove*. Milly, unlike Isabel and Maggie, or even Strether, is not
allowed to strike through her pasteboard mask. Her tragedy builds to
a climax when she realizes that, even when she is ready to break
through romance, Death, Densher, Kate, and Lord Mark are unwill-

ing to let her become real. She must continue to be a priestess, a dove, a Bronzino portrait. She herself is concerned about how "a dove *would* act." [89] James allows Milly to play only verbally upon the possibilities of consummating relationship before romance closes her up again in isolation. In a very moving meditation in Venice before Lord Mark who, like Osmond, persists in viewing the heroine as portrait, Milly reflects upon the tragic paradoxes of romance:

> Oh, the impossible romance! The romance for her, yet once more, would be to sit there for ever, through all her time, as in a fortress; and the idea became an image of never going down, of remaining aloft in the divine, dustless air, where she would hear but the plash of the water against the stone. The great floor on which they moved was at an altitude, and this prompted the rueful fancy. "Ah, not to go down—never, never to go down" she strangely sighed to her friend. (II, 147)

Milly does not complete the traditional Jamesian launching into the waters of relationship, but she guides posthumously "the ark of her deluge" (II, 143). Her only possible release is in ritual, as the dove bearing the twig of life back to the ark filled with couples. Her closest friend, Susan Stringham (who like the others is guilty of prolonging Milly's "pictorial" life), senses the portrait Death makes of her and the poignancy of her happiness:

> "She's lodged for the first time as she ought, from her type, to be; and doing it—I mean bringing out all the glory of the place— makes her really happy. It's a Veronese picture, as near as can be— with me as the inevitable dwarf, the small blackamoor, put into a corner of the foreground for effect. If I only had a hawk or a hound or something of that sort I should do the scene more honour." (II, 206)

The religious context of the picture isolates Milly all the more in the loneliness of martyrdom.[40]

James himself deliberately persists in seeing Milly, whenever she is in contact with an apparently vibrant force, as picture. His imagistic play, at moments like the following in which he seems to set Kate upon Milly, presages the play in which Maggie's mind abounds in the second part of *The Golden Bowl* when she is circling her antagonist and actively shifting the burden (and salvation) of a picture-life from her own shoulders to those of Charlotte:

Certain aspects of the connection of these young women show for us, such is the twilight that gathers about them, in the likeness of some dim scene in a Maeterlinck play; we have positively the image, in the delicate dusk, of the figures so associated and yet so opposed, so mutually watchful: that of the angular, pale princess, ostrich-plumed, black robed, hung about with amulets, reminders, relics, mainly seated, mainly still, and that of the upright, restless slow-circling lady of her court, who exchanges with her, across the black water streaked with evening gleams, fitful questions and answers. The upright lady, with thick, dark braids down her back, drawing over the grass a more embroidered train, makes the whole circuit, and makes it again, and the broken talk, brief and sparingly allusive, seems more to cover than to free their sense. (II, 139)

Whereas Maggie stalks to free herself from Charlotte's framing and graciously to save her warden, Kate's encaging of Milly ironically requires the permanent containment of the warden. This instance of irony is not unique. Consistently in James the determinism of the pictured state is fostered by both the romantic and the naturalistic vision. James goes to great pains in his preface to *The Wings of the Dove* [41] to show that, whereas neither Milly nor Kate in the individual case is fixed or fated, much in the relationship is determined by the romance of Milly's freedom (her fate) and by the family background of Kate that has "tampered with her springs." The struggle is always that of the object, the seen character, toward elevation to subject, and the new equilibrium usually demands a simultaneous reduction (Madame Merle, Chad, Kate, Charlotte) elsewhere on the scene. Only hero and heroine are chosen to fulfill the challenge of expanding consciousness, even if it only turns the face to the wall.

IV Centers of Consciousness: The Capacity for Relationship

Edgar of Ravenswood . . . visited by the tragic tempest of "The Bride of Lammermoor," has a black cloak and hat and feathers more than he has a mind.[1]

Henry James

The critics who have recognized the carefully controlled center of consciousness as James's greatest contribution to the shaping of the modern novel have generally relegated it, in their discussions, to the camp of craft. Yet this contribution is as crucial for the development of moral substance and weight in the novel as for its stylistic form. Particularly in the late and major James there is a clear identity between center of consciousness and capacity for relationship. James's most consistent irony depends upon the assumption that full consciousness is not bestowed arbitrarily upon character, but that the character earns it through stages of honest bewilderment. Until the romantic ghosts are actively exorcised (none of James's genuine heroes begins like Austen's Emma, as a shaper of the human personality) major consciousness is merely a dormant malady. It takes a lot of exposure before the chosen vessels understand how their creator has made them different from the others. Their superior consciousness must convince us of their superior morality and also of their superior realism. James traces the evolution of conscious responsibility not only by concentration on the individual case, but by surrounding that case with characters who remain objects or whose vision, even with good intentions, remains that of the connoisseur. (We should point out here that since James's short stories are often diagrammatic condensations of the themes that are deepened and developed in the novels, "The Real Thing" might be considered a map for the tragedy of object posing as subject, costume as mind, "fool" as "free agent.")

Both the overestimation of personality and its objectification which are integral to the romantic vision mean, we have said, the substitution, even in the self, of a role for relationship. T. S. Eliot's remarks on Othello who "succeeds in turning himself into a pathetic figure, by adopting an aesthetic rather than a moral attitude, dramatizing himself against his environment" [2] are, with Fyodor Pavlovitch Karamazov's own words about himself, significant affirmations of the danger of this substitution if it is allowed full rein. But the mature James heroine is commissioned to break through the isolationism which permits the aesthetic to control our concepts of reality. When a major character avoids the burdens of consciousness and control, he lives through his costume rather than his mind:

> Edgar of Ravenswood for instance, visited by the tragic tempest of "The Bride of Lammermoor," has a black cloak and hat and feathers more than he has a mind; just as Hamlet, while equally sabled and draped and plumed, while at least equally romantic, has yet a mind still more than he has a costume. The situation represented is that Ravenswood loves Lucy Ashton through dire difficulty and danger, and that she in the same way loves him; but the relation so created between them is by this neglect of the "feeling" question never shown us as primarily taking place. It is shown only in its secondary, its confused and disfigured aspects. . . . The thing has . . . paid for its deviation . . . by a sacrifice of intensity. . . .[3]

(This is, appropriately, the opera to which Madame Bovary responds so fully.) Against the encumbrance of costume James pictures the freedom of bare feet. His autobiography, which, like his novels, is largely dominated by the struggle between the fixed and the free, is directed by this image of freedom:

> They were to become great and beautiful, the household of that glimmering vision, they were to figure historically, heroically, and serve great public ends; but always, to my remembering eyes and fond fancy, they were to move through life as with the bare white feet of that original preferred fairness and wildness.[4]

Heroic stature is not the assumption of historical costume, but the shining display of honest nakedness. In his most mature novels James consistently implies that only with the acceptance of the risks of consciousness, can the riches that come with real freedom emerge. It is ironically when Isabel, Strether, Milly, and Maggie feel (without understanding) most bare-footed, most carefree, that they most

resemble Edgar of Ravenswood. In that state, freedom is only enslavement in disguise. They make freedom meaningful only when
they come to terms with the terror of nakedness, as well as the joy,
when they consciously abandon the costume for the mind. The James
child-heroine is not burdened by the historical or psychological rebellion against the father. James has granted her freedom and has
forced her toward the temptations of choosing roles.

One of James's favorite paradoxes develops when role and costume
choose the heroine. Often the James subject grows into a counter-
revolutionary stage in which the father is sought rather than rejected.
Only Maggie must cut herself off from her father, and the softness
of her gestures reveals how little an act of rebellion it is. It is rather
an adjustment, and the terror of detachment on both sides is absorbed
by marriage.

Naturally, such consciousness can be granted only to those with
capacities to work it. The problem of the laboring, suffering, re-
nouncing subject surrounded by the lures of the object world and its
comfortable vision is materially obvious in *The Spoils of Poynton*
(1897), which, like *The Portrait* and *What Maisie Knew* heralds the
late novels. James worried the problem in his preface to that novel:

> One is confronted obviously thus with the question of the im-
> portances; with that in particular, no doubt, of the weight of
> intelligent consciousness, consciousness of the whole, or of some-
> thing ominously like it, that one may decently permit a represented
> figure to appear to throw. Some plea for this cause, that of the
> intelligence of the moved mannikin, I have already had occasion
> to make, and can scarce hope too often to evade it. This intelli-
> gence, an honourable amount of it, on the part of the person to
> whom one most invited attention, has but to play with sufficient
> freedom and ease, or call it with the right grace, to guarantee us
> that quantum of the impression of beauty which is the most fixed
> of the possible advantages of our producible effect. It may fail, as
> a positive presence, on other sides and in other connexions; but
> more or less of the treasure is stored safe from the moment such a
> quality of inward life is distilled, or in other words from the
> moment so fine an interpretation and criticism as that of Fleda
> Vetch's—to cite the present case—is applied without waste to the
> surrounding tangle.[5]

The necessary "quality of bewilderment," intelligence, and application, which guarantees the proper dimension to the heroine in
the face of the object world has its source, as always, in the sympa-

thetic attachment of author to subject, for, as James suggests in the preface to *The Princess Casamassima,* if the sensitive novelist himself cannot direct his prepared consciousness to meet the world's possibilities, he, like his flat characters, becomes a fool:

> What it all came back to was, no doubt, something like *this* wisdom—that if you haven't, for fiction, the root of the matter in you, haven't the sense of life and the penetrating imagination, you are a fool in the very presence of the revealed and assured; but that if you *are* so armed you are not really helpless without your resource, even before mysteries abysmal.[6]

A free spirit struggling to work out its life is potentially heroic as it engages in the process of directing its conscious attention toward the tangle of objects and fools before it. The burden of bearing the greatest conscious capacity on the scene isolates the subject, at crucial moments, as surely as formal tragedy. There is no greater disparity in James than between his vessels of consciousness and the connoisseurs of vessels, between the smugness of aesthetic knowing and the discomforts of moral exploration; it is this disparity which so often marks his drama of "renunciation." The subject must learn what the object world knows, but that is only the beginning of wisdom. Fleda Vetch, unlike the heroines of James's greatest novels of moral drama, though still a partial victim of her own innocence, has from the beginning a relatively steady degree of high consciousness and appreciation and has, consequently, much less growing to do. The tragedy of isolation from real relationship which attends her superiority is determined not so much by her own false vision, as by the unconscious materiality of the tangle of views surrounding hers. James saw the whole novel in terms of this spirit bounded by the material, and his title, like the title of Isabel Archer's drama, is indicative of his determination to separate subject from object:

> From beginning to end, in "The Spoils of Poynton," appreciation, even to that of the very whole, lives in Fleda; which is precisely why, as a consequence rather grandly imposed, every one else shows for comparatively stupid; the tangle, the drama, the tragedy and comedy of those who appreciate consisting so much of their relation with those who don't. . . . The "things" are radiant, shedding afar, with a merciless monotony, all their light, exerting their ravage without remorse; and Fleda almost demonically both sees and feels, while the others but feel without seeing. Thus we get perhaps a vivid enough little example, in the concrete, of the

general truth, for the spectator of life, that the fixed constituents of almost any reproducible action are the fools who minister, at a particular crisis, to the intensity of the free spirit engaged with them. The fools are interesting by contrast, by the salience they acquire, and by a hundred other of their advantages; and the free spirit, always much tormented, and by no means always triumphant, is heroic, ironic, pathetic or whatever, and, as exemplified in the record of Fleda Vetch, for instance, "successful," only through having remained free.[7]

James is intrigued by the possible degrees of freedom and grace, short of the torturing gift of deep consciousness, he can grant to his "surrounding" characters. (The game he plays in *The Spoils* is more explicitly indulged in *The Sacred Fount*.) Mrs. Gereth, for example, is in many ways the reverse of a free spirit and her apparent cleverness is less perceptive than Mrs. Assingham's intelligence:

> Mrs. Gereth was, obviously, with her pride and her pluck, of an admirable paste; but she was not intelligent, was only clever, and therefore could have been no use to us at all as centre of our subject—compared with Fleda, who was only intelligent, not distinctly able.[8]

It is, of course, one of James's supreme ironies, that those who worship the world of objects can attach themselves easily to the subjects, while the subjects, who have only the finest, not the most manipulative, intelligence, are tragically isolated unless their vision, like that of the matured Maggie, can reform an object of attachment into a subject. Fleda and Strether have really nothing to work on; they are bound neither by ceremony like Isabel nor by tried love like Maggie. Social action is, of course, much easier for those who live in the world of objects, for the absence of true relationship means that passion, desire, or even anger can substitute for love, that there is no need for subtle directions. Of his character Mona Brigstock, James writes:

> She loses no minute in that perception of incongruities in which half Fleda's passion is wasted and misled, and into which Mrs. Gereth, to her practical loss, that is by the fatal grace of a sense of comedy, occasionally and disinterestedly strays.[9]

This shallowness makes it easy for the fools to use the heroines in a way that would be impossible in a reversed position. Mrs. Gereth commits the unpardonable sin with "unconscious brutality and immorality." [10] This kind of immorality is possible, of course, only when relationship and morality are not rising together but are split apart. (The latter course would indicate that a relationship was only apparent.) How much Mrs. Gereth thinks of Fleda herself in terms of the object world, the world of manipulation, and not in terms of relationship, the world of respect, is evidenced by James's note: *"She sets the girl on him."* He continues: "cynically, almost, or indecently (making her feel AGAIN how little account—in the way of fine respect—she makes of her)." [11]

This is one of the major problems of the James subject, that its great freedom opens it to manipulation by the object. But there is, we have seen, an even greater risk in James's fuller heroines. Isabel, Maggie, Milly, and Strether have in addition, their own romantic visions to cope with, and are also open to the risks of ignorance or self-deception, and because of this vulnerability, they themselves are often manipulators, of a very different sort. Each "victim" forces the action by ignorance (or, more accurately, innocence) and the willingness to overrate. When the shift in knowledge is effected, which is also a shift in power, as it is in the major late novels and in novels like *The Portrait of a Lady, What Maisie Knew,* and *The Awkward Age* (though the latter two, using rather unique devices of the child's consciousness and the predominance of dialogue, are not really as relevant to our discussion as *The Portrait*), then the heroines are explicitly manipulators recomposing lives and relationships. They are metamorphic in a way that Fleda never needs to be, for their heroic triumphs and renunciations are based upon adjustment in their own vision. Fleda's rather static tragedy evolves as the object world works on the immobile subject world, but the victories of Isabel, Milly, Strether, and Maggie, though at times Pyrrhic, develop as the subject world works on the object world and makes the object a subject, whether it be in relation to itself or to others.

This was the great challenge that James placed before the novelist and consequently before character as well: render the center of consciousness totally "disponible" so that the choosing of relationship transforms conventional morality into the morality of love. It is this desire that explains the depression that Isabel, Milly, and Maggie feel at points of turning in their lives; it is not caused by the mere fact of the realization that they have been exploited. When Don Quixote becomes in the second part of his novel a literary character to the world he once controlled by his imagination, when his private power of illusion becomes public property, when he becomes an object of play for the Duke and the Duchess, when his imagination is forcefed rather than self-creating, then debilitating depression seizes the hero. Isabel, Milly, and Maggie all recognize at some point that they themselves have been feeding the process of objectifying their own personalities; they all pass through the humiliation of seeing their imagined free and powerful dreams of life played with and debased by those who supposedly love them. All reject the privilege of vengeance and base profit. James bestows upon them instead the duties of spiritual and emotional salvation—an ironic climax to the life of the young and the innocent American who was to be saved by Europe experientially and socially. James's own equal fascination and sense of risk in the face of the establishment of character as unknowing subject and knowing savior, as a strong center of consciousness, is displayed in his notes about his first great heroine, Isabel Archer. He wonders:

> By what process of logical accretion was this slight "personality," the mere slim shade of an intelligent but presumptuous girl, to find itself endowed with the high attributes of a Subject?—and indeed by what thinness, at the best, would such a subject not be vitiated? Millions of presumptuous girls, intelligent or not intelligent, daily affront their destiny, and what is it open to their destiny to *be*, at the most, that we should make an ado about it? The novel is of its very nature an "ado," an ado about something, and the larger the form it takes the greater of course the ado. Therefore, consciously, that was what one was in for—for positively organizing an ado about Isabel Archer. . . .[12]

There was hardly a challenge in the whole of the novelistic process which appealed more to James than this of the vulnerability of his "frail vessel of consciousness," of the actual loosening of structural or societal supports around it (supports like set manners,[13] shared consciousness in the subplotting or comic relief, which bolstered so many heroes and heroines from Shakespeare to George Eliot), so that the vessel might be for itself "sole minister of its appeal."[14] Then, and only then, could relationship, carrying a full cargo, sail from that center and back to it with an even richer weight. Only in this way could leakage in consciousness be supremely minimized. James cuts behind him all the bridges of evasion "for retreat and flight" which George Eliot was willing to construct out of the sub-relations surrounding her heroines. His plan was more "difficult":

"Place the centre of the subject in the young woman's own con-
sciouness," I said to myself, "and you get as interesting and as
beautiful a difficulty as you could wish. Stick to *that* for the centre; put the heaviest weight into *that* scale, which will be so largely
the scale of her relation to herself. Make her only interested
enough, at the same time, in the things that are not herself, and
this relation needn't fear to be too limited. Place meanwhile in the
other scale the lighter weight (which is usually the one that
tips the balance of interest): press least hard, in short, on the consciousness of your heroine's satellites, especially the male; make it
an interest contributive only to the greater one.[15]

Once created, the James heroine grows to understand Adam's
curse, and his blessing, that she "must labour to be beautiful." We
have prefigured here the same danger which Lawrence equated with
putting the thumb in the pan, though in a different guise. The old
novel "failed" to centralize and concentrate consciousness to that
point at which relationship contains and registers the fullest moral
possibilities. The development of the James novel of relationship depends upon a firm and free center of consciousness which does not
fix by naming the subjects of the world, but which discovers their
fluidity in the act of relating, thus deliberately forcing moral judgment to complexity. No artist of the novel before James (despite
severe control) ever trusted his characters so much to work out
standards of morality by working out centers of relationship; he
never lost his feeling that his "relation of confidence with the
actors in (his) drama who *were,* unlike Miss Stackpole, true agents,
was an excellent one to have arrived at" [16] and one which laid the
groundwork for his relation with the reader.

What this trust between James and his character comes to is simply the self-assurance on the part of the author that he has granted
to his vessel the proper weight of intelligence, moral sense, and, at
the same time, *"quality* of bewilderment" [17] to confirm its complexity. The vessel must be a free spirit instead of a fool, a subject instead of an object, a capacity instead of a limitation:

Verily even, I think the "story" is possible without its fools. . . .
At the same time I confess I never see the *leading* interest of any
human hazard but in a consciousness (on the part of the moved
and moving creature) subject to fine intensification and wide enlargement. . . . This means, exactly, that the person capable of
feeling in the given case more than another of what is to be felt
for it, and so serving in the highest degree to *record* it dra-

matically and objectively, is the only sort of person on whom we can count not to betray, to cheapen or, as we say, give away, the value and beauty of the thing.[18]

This responsibility demands the painful sacrifice of "the straight vindictive view, the rights of resentment, the rages of jealously, the protests of passion." [19] Eventually, freedom and control come together with the impression that the freedom is controlled by character itself. The means for the exploitation and direction of freedom is manifested in character as, in James's words, "a considerable capacity for conduct." [20] This capacity by no means contradicts the tremendous freedom granted character in James, but, on the contrary, guarantees the benefits of this freedom, makes it work, and finally prevents it from being arbitrary.

It is precisely this absence of home-rule that James found so distasteful in the French naturalistic novels, particularly those of Maupassant and Zola. On the other hand, it is in a novelist like Turgenev that James sees the conception of feminine heroism that he admires, the heroism that reveals itself in "strength of will—the power to resist, to wait, to attain," the power to determine and to act,[21] a function that Turgenev's heroes so often relinquish. One immediately thinks in the English novel of Eliot's Dorothea. Nevertheless, James spotted in Dorothea's role a weakness which detracted from the general force of the novel about her:

> Dorothea was altogether too superb a heroine to be wasted; yet she plays a narrower part than the imagination of the reader demands. She is of more consequence than the action of which she is the nominal centre.[22]

And because the histories of Dorothea and Gwendolen Harleth are deliberately dwarfed by the vast stage with which the author leaves us, the final choice of direction, the personal fate, is limited by a universal fate. In his dialogue on *Daniel Deronda,* James has Constantius observe of the novel:

> The universe forcing itself with a slow, inexorable pressure into a narrow, complacent, and yet after all extremely sensitive mind, and making it ache with the pain of the process—this is Gwendolen's story. And it becomes completely characteristic in that her supreme perception of the fact that the world is whirling past her is in the disappointment not of a base but of an exalted passion. The very chance to embrace what the author is so fond of calling

a "larger life" seems refused to her. She is punished for being narrow, and she is not allowed a chance to expand. Her finding Deronda pre-engaged to go to the East and stir up the race-feeling of the Jews strikes me as a wonderfully happy invention. The irony of the situation, for poor Gwendolen, is almost grotesque, and it makes one wonder whether the whole heavy structure of the Jewish question in the story was not built up by the author for the express purpose of giving its proper force to this particular stroke.[23]

Despite his great admiration for Eliot, James was always nettled by her unwillingness to trust her characters as completely as he did his. For free relationship to shape morality, the hero must have, with the capacity for conduct, the "capacity to be tempted." The Fall was always for James imbedded deep in the conscience of his great heroines, and the capacity for conduct, which implies a capacity for choice and judgment, is meaningless without the possibilities of wrong choice. Environmental influence might have narrowed choice for Gwendolen and Dorothea, but they are certainly vulnerable to temptation. Eliot's hero of romance, Adam Bede, is to James's mind a stiff and boring character, ruled by preconceived standards of morality and a fixed society; he is conduct itself rather than the capacity for conduct. His choices are not really free, so his relationships are not real:

> My chief complaint with Adam Bede himself is that he is too good. He is meant, I conceive, to be every inch a man; but to my mind, there are several inches wanting. He lacks spontaneity and sensibility, he is too stiff-backed. He lacks that supreme quality without which a man can never be interesting to men,—the capacity to be tempted. His nature is without richness or responsiveness. . . .[24]

The distance between Eliot and James can be measured by the distance between Adam Bede and Strether. Strether's discipline is not the fulfillment of New England morality, but rather the finding of a new morality in the breakthrough to relationship. This is the subject that interested James. Of course, Strether is not from the start *meant* to be "every inch a man," but he must convince us that his sad heroism is significant and valid despite the fact that he lives through others:

> The whole thing is, of course, to intensity, a picture of relations— and among them, though not on the first line, the relation of

Strether to Chad. The relation of Chad to Strether is a limited and according to my method only implied and indicated thing, sufficiently there; but Strether's to Chad consists above all in a charmed and yearning and wondering sense, a dimly envious sense, of all Chad's young living and easily-taken other relations; other not only than the one to him, but than the one to Mme de Vionnet and whoever else; this very sense, and the sense of Chad, generally, is a part, a large part, of poor dear Strether's discipline, development, adventure and general history.[25]

This kind of development is possible only because relationship radiates not from separated centers, but from Strether himself. Without the mind of Strether, the story of Chad and Mme de Vionnet is essentially conventional. While James saw in Eliot a dissipation through lack of centralization, or a blocking by the substitution of conduct for the capacity for conduct, in the French novelists whom he most admired he saw, with more acute anxiety, the dangers of limited consciousness for the possibilities of relationship.

He complained about the mere pretense of cultivated consciousness in Balzac's characters:

> His truest and vividest people are those whom the conditions in which they are so palpably embedded have simplified not less than emphasized; simplified mostly to singleness of motive and passion and interest, to quite measurably finite existence; whereas his ostensibly higher spirits, types necessarily least observed and most independently thought out, in the interest of their humanity, as we would fain ourselves think them, are his falsest and weakest and show most where his imagination and his efficient sympathy break down.[26]

If Balzac's characters too often have depth by imputation and substance by allegation, Flaubert's have not even the advantage of authorial ambition. Emma, unlike Fleda Vetch, has no means to deal with the world of objects and a heroism of renunciation would be an empty one without consciousness:

> Emma Bovary's poor adventures are a tragedy for the very reason that in a world unsuspecting, unassisting, unconsoling, she has herself to distil the rich and the rare. Ignorant, unguided, undiverted, ridden by the very nature and mixture of her consciousness, she makes of the business an inordinate failure, a failure which in its turn makes for Flaubert the most pointed, the most *told* of anecdotes.[27]

[*89*]

We have seen how James related the poverty of Emma's mind to that of Flaubert's lack of projection of "efficient sympathy." The deliberate distancing by persistent irony between author and hero in both *Madame Bovary* and *L'Education sentimentale* is a device which allows for the mocking of rhetorics (of love, of knowledge, of art, of revolution) and refuses the persuasive power of true soliloquy; obviously, it could not satisfy James's need for engagement. The most "told" of anecdotes fails to be the most "felt" of stories. But granting Flaubert's scale of "middling experience" Emma fails, with Frédéric, to satisfy in yet another way. Because consciousness in the major subject is of a poor quality, representational power is reduced. Since Emma and Frédéric relate so meagerly to others and to themselves, their capacity for representative extension is poorer, because of our heroic expectations, than that of the fools who at least enjoy vivid and specific caricature. James is forced to ask of Emma:

> Representative of what? . . . The plea for her is the plea made for all the figures that live without evaporation under the painter's hand—that they are not only particular persons but types of their kind, and as valid in one light as in the other. It is Emma's "kind" that I question for this responsibility, even if it be inquired of me why I then fail to question that of Charles Bovary, in its perfection, or that of the inimitable, the immortal Homais. If we express Emma's deficiency as the poverty of her consciousness for the typical function, it is certainly not, one must admit, that she is surpassed in this respect either by her platitudinous husband or by his friend the pretentious apothecary. The difference is none the less somehow in the fact that they are respectivly studies but of their character and office, which function in each expresses adequately *all* they are. . . . Emma is the same for myself, I plead; she is conditioned to such an excess of the specific, and the specific in her case leaves out so many even of the commoner elements of conceivable life in a woman when we are invited to see that life as pathetic, as dramatic agitation, that we challenge both the author's and the critic's scale of importances.[28]

Even her small social significance is "greater on the whole than her capacity for consciousness," and it is the capacity for consciousness that determines both the power of her relationships and of her representation: "we feel her less illustrational than she might have been not only if the world had offered her more points of contact, but if she had had more of these to give it." [29]

We could hardly expect James to find Emma morally interesting when her relationships can be of the most superficial romanticism. Gwendolen Harleth is driven, when her major relationship is cut off by the structural dissipation of the novel's center of consciousness and by the clarification of Deronda's direction, to the expression of an established Christian morality, to the desire to "be better." We know this is not the Jamesian solution, but it is a moral choice, and her words are those of his suffering heroine, Isabel Archer: "I shall live. I mean to live." [30] Emma, on the other hand, is so bankrupt of conscience that she has only the amorality of suicide to turn to, and this choice, or lack of choice, would be inconceivable to James. *The Portrait of a Lady* might be considered, then, as a severer "correction" of Flaubert than of Eliot; Isabel, like Emma, has falsified relationship by her romantic vision, but because she has the capacity for conduct and consciousness and the courage for metamorphosis, disillusionment forces her back to life. For Emma there is no breakthrough, and disillusionment to a limited register can only mean a blank death. (The disillusionment of a sensitive register like Hyacinth Robinson makes an interesting contrast. Here suicide, so rare in James, is, of course, an heroic moral choice.) Ralph's last words to Isabel are: "Dear Isabel, life is better; for in life there's love. Death is good—but there's no love." [31]

It is a mistake to think of Isabel's choice as renunciation. Surely it is James's reverence for consciousness that makes him so affirmative for life. To a friend in despair James wrote movingly:

> Consciousness is an illimitable power, and though at times it may seem to be all consciousness of misery, yet in the way it propagates itself from wave to wave, so that we never cease to feel, and though at moments we appear to, try to, pray to, there is something that holds one in one's place, makes it a standpoint in the universe which it is probably good not to forsake.[32]

This is his letter to Isabel.

In *Madame Bovary* the genius of Flaubert has somehow managed to forge a masterpiece out of the subject of mediocrity. But *L'Education sentimentale* cannot overcome the burden of its small central intelligence. Absence of the author's respect for the mind of the hero leaves this novel ultimately "a curiosity for a literary museum." [33] The balloons of experience are never cut loose:

> [The novel] affects us as an epic without air, without wings to lift it; reminds us in fact more than anything else of a huge

balloon, all of silk pieces strongly sewn together and patiently blown up, but that absolutely refuses to leave the ground.[34]

Mme Arnoux might have been a Mme de Vionnet or spread wings of the dove, but she is bound to the ground by Frédéric's poor vision and her own bourgeois limitations. Repeatedly James implies that this smallness has not only aesthetic but ethical consequences. What James cannot forgive is, not just the willful limitation of consciousness in character (after all, the depth of character is a privilege of its creator), but the suspicion of complacent blindness in Flaubert himself:

> What *was* compromising—and the great point is that it remained so, that nothing has an equal weight against it—is the unconsciousness of error in respect to the opportunity that would have counted as his finest. We feel not so much that Flaubert misses it, for that we could bear; but that he doesn't *know* he misses it is what stamps the blunder. We do not pretend to say how he might have shown us Madame Arnoux better—that was his own affair. What is ours is that he really thought he was showing her as well as he could, or as she might be shown; at which we veil our face.[35]

Most readers of Flaubert would question this assumption of his ignorance since Madame Arnoux calls herself "bourgeoise." We are always asked, it seems to me, to bring to Flaubert's "bourgeois" novels the double recognition that Emma and Frédéric are victims of their place and times (provinces and bourgeois monarchy) though surely not tragic victims, while they are, at the same time, victims of their own mediocrity. Discovering the worst about life and love, about inevitable deception and disappointment, does not help the self to achieve the best. On the contrary, Emma and Frédéric are perfectly willing to yield their "density" to life's floods, to death or *"le hasard."* James did not concern himself with Flaubert's historical excuse, and he could not forgive the blight of such soulless and cowardly, such determined registers. We can see by this reaction how "anti-realistic" in the traditional sense James actually was, how much closer he was to the old heroism than to the new anti-hero. The anachronism of this preference is possibly what forced him into the world of romance.

Though Hardy's ironic vision is of a blunter sort, he too, by limiting the range of consciousness in his characters, keeps his balloon anchored:

This is Mr. Hardy's trouble; he rarely gets beyond ambitious artifice—the mechanical stimulation of heat and depth and wisdom that are absent. Farmer Boldwood is a shadow, and Sergeant Troy an elaborate stage-figure. Everything human in the book strikes us as factitious and insubstantial; the only things we believe in are the sheep and the dogs.[36]

It is this vision, like Maupassant's, that turns tragedy into pathos. As Lawrence states in his frequently brilliant piece on Hardy, his characters are "one year's accidental crop." [37] In the "pagan" worlds of Maupassant and Hardy neither Christianity nor any confessional strain of deep consciousness has interiorized fate, so heavy irony keeps the picture distant.

For James and Lawrence, of course, fate was always an intimate outgrowth of consciousness, and exploratory thrusts of irony which temporarily separate author from major character are gradually obliterated by the "efficient sympathy" between cause and direction in author and character. The sense of universe in Hardy's setting appealed to Lawrence, of course, more than to James, for Lawrence's own Odyssean circuit spread out to the heaths of the world. But relationship is inevitably mocked by unremitting irony and the outer circle of the universe was still a response to the inner circle of a character's sensibility, or vice versa. For all his diatribes against white consciousness, Lawrence was much closer in his relational patterns to James than he was to the ironic shadows of Hardy's world. He was not put off by major centers of consciousness; these could be refined and directed by the novelist towards a blood consciousness, as drama and particular personality were expanded into poem and pure relationship. But he did object to the "democratic" distribution of consciousness, as in the Russian novels, which exposes us to the "phenomenal coruscations of the souls of quite commonplace people." [38] It was not the heroism of consciousness that Lawrence rejected for his major characters, but the static sickness of self-consciousness.

The novel that closes the worlds of relationship, whether personal or universal, was as annoying to Lawrence as it was to James. It is an anguishing vision of Hardy's that limits the possibilities of relatedness by inexorably maintaining the ironic split between "the vast, unexplored morality of life itself, what we call the immorality of nature" and the inner "little human morality play." [39] In distinguishing Hardy's view from that of Shakespeare and Sophocles, Lawrence perceptively observes:

Whereas in Shakespeare or Sophocles the greater, uncomprehended morality, or fate, is actively transgressed and gives active punishment, in Hardy and Tolstoi the lesser, human morality, the mechanical system is actively transgressed, and holds, and punishes the protagonist, whilst the greater morality is only passively, negatively transgressed, it is represented merely as being present in background, in scenery, not taking any active part, having no direct connexion with the protagonist.[40]

In Laurentian terms, there is in Hardy no reconciliation between Love and Law.[41] In Hardy's world Love is killed by Law that cannot be balanced in relationship, but which isolates instead without yielding tragedy. Lawrence and James were distressed by Flaubert's and Hardy's ironic visions which reduced and isolated character and made pathetic a poor or paralyzed consciousness. In different ways, Flaubert and Hardy (with Lawrence's Tolstoi) are death-oriented.

The personal complex that causes ambivalence, repression, and distortion in the communication between author and characters and which finally results in a regretfully stunted projection of "felt life" is described by James (in his case against Flaubert) and by Lawrence (in his case against Hardy). But even for the sake of the new perspective that realignment gives us, we cannot pretend that the alliance of Lawrence and James can lead us very far. Surely we could never call Lawrence what Conrad called James, "the historian of fine consciences." [42] And James is never willing to "sacrifice" the circumference of the novel to the infiniteness of the universe. In the preface to *Roderick Hudson,* James had noted: "Really, universally, relations stop nowhere, and the exquisite problem of the artist is eternally but to draw, by a geometry of his own, the circle within which they shall happily *appear* to do so." [43] It is within this smaller circle that the fine conscience is examined, yet in his greatest works, James, honoring the infinity of relationship, does leave open ends. In his florid appreciation of James, Conrad perhaps gives us the reason for the impression James gives of real life:

And, indeed, ugliness has but little place in this world of his creation. Yet it is always felt in the truthfulness of his art; it is there, it surrounds the scene, it presses close upon it; it is made visible, tangible, in the struggles, in the contacts of the fine consciences, in their perplexities, in the sophism of their mistakes. For a fine conscience is naturally a virtuous one. What is natural about it is just its fineness, and abiding sense of the intangible, ever-present, right. It is most visible in their ultimate triumph, in their emergence from miracle, through an energetic act of renunciation.[44]

The fine conscience at the center of a dynamic relationship, in short, prevents the James novel from closing its circumference with a *deus ex machina*. But it would be perhaps more accurate to stress the positive side of choice in James. It is not actually renunciation that keeps the novel open; it is rather James's reverence for the love which engages the fine conscience in the morality of relationship. James would have subscribed to these words of Santayana on Dante's characters, Francesca and Paolo, though he would have carefully defined the implications of "unlawful":

> Love itself dreams of more than mere possession; to conceive happiness, it must conceive a life to be shared in a varied world, full of events and activities, which shall be new and ideal bonds between the lovers. But unlawful love cannot pass out into this public fulfillment. It is condemned to mere possession—possession in the dark, without an environment, without a future. It is love among the ruins. . . . Abandon yourself . . . altogether to a love that is nothing but love, and you are in hell already.[45]

Because the James consciousness cannot expand in a social vacuum, commitment to a relationship cannot be a private affair. The unions of the Prince and Charlotte Stant, of Merton Densher and Kate Croy are destroyed when exposed to the life and the love of the daytime. Secrecy did not preserve relationship, but only prevented a finer one from flowering. In James it is not social law but the quality and metaphysic of love as it lives in the social world that save and condemn. The social "unlawfulness" of the union of the Prince and Charlotte symbolizes the emotional "unlawfulness" of their romantic attachment as truly as Clifford Chatterley's actual paralysis symbolizes his spiritual paralysis. The isolation of relationship has graver consequences than adultery itself, for it is, after all, the fullness of relationship, not its technical legality that determines Jamesian morality, and Mme de Vionnet and Chad had a "virtuous attachment."

James's so-called prudery has by now been sufficiently and subtly enough discussed to prevent easy condemnation.[46] Dorothea Krook, who convincingly explains the consistency of Isabel's fear of passion, claims that in the novels of the late period, James's "life experience" helped him to correct the earlier "tragic error" by showing "the power of sexual passion to redeem (as well as destroy)." This lesson, claims Miss Krook, is "exhibited with a fullness of knowledge to be found nowhere else in the English novel." [47] If we feel at times his experiential weakness, we can at least admit that his imaginative sympathy effects an intensity in the man-woman engagement that projects the pressures of real sexual attachment. As a critic James never turned away from the use of the sexual motif in the novel, but he was always firm in condemning the abuse of the sexual allusion which made a farce of relationship, and though his fervency was never exposed or frenzied like Lawrence's, even in this area, the two novelists shared basic assumptions and beliefs.

᥉ V Boots in the Hall:
Sex in Relationship

The lovers are naked in the market-place and perform for
the benefit of society. The matter with them, to the perception
of the stupified spectator, is that they entertained for each
other every feeling in life but the feeling of respect. What the
absence of that article may do for the passion of hate is apparently nothing to what it may do for the passion of love.[1]
                                                    Henry James

James's most central discussion of the actual use of sex in the
novel, of its necessary subsumption under the major plan of relationship, is undertaken in his essays on D'Annunzio. The isolationism of
that novelist's sensual texture (which served as well for theme),
was to James's mind as unhealthy as the hypocrisy of pornography
that so irritated Lawrence:

That sexual passion from which he extracts with admirable detached pictures insists on remaining for him *only* the act of a
moment, beginning and ending in itself and disowning any representative character. From the moment it depends on itself alone
for its beauty it endangers extremely its distinction, so precarious
at the best. For what it represents, precisely, is it poetically interesting; it finds its extension and consummation only in the rest of
life. Shut out from the rest of life, shut out from all fruition and
assimilation, it has no more dignity than—to use a homely image
—the boots and shoes that we see, in the corridors of promiscuous
hotels, standing, often in double pairs, at the doors of rooms. Detached and unassociated these clusters of objects present, however
obtruded, no importance.[2]

[97]

This exclusive sexual passion, divorced from the larger circuit of relationship, relinquishes dignity, and, like Paolo and Francesca, those characters who embody it are in hell:

> What the participants do with their agitation, in short, or even what it does with them, that is the stuff of poetry, and it is never really interesting save when something finely contributive in themselves makes it so. It is this absence of anything finely contributive in themselves, on the part of the various couples here concerned, that is the open door to the trivial. I have said, with all appreciation, that they present the great "relation," for intimacy, as we shall nowhere else find it presented; but to see it related, in its own turn, to nothing in the heaven above or the earth beneath, this undermines, we definitely learn, the charm of that achievement.[3]

The crudest detractors of Lawrence's novels will readily apply this criticism to him. It certainly would not have been enough for either Lawrence or James, to stop at such limited meaning of theme that could so casually be summed up as: "There is an inevitable leak of ease and peace when a mistress happens to be considerably older than her lover." [4] The love relationship pushes theme beyond this emotional cartoon. Both James and Lawrence warned, either explicitly or implicitly, against the decay of sex into counterfeit love. James vehemently censures the static counterfeiting of D'Annunzio's novels:

> It is throughout one of D'Annunzio's strongest marks that he treats "love" as a matter not to be mixed with life, in the larger sense of the word, at all—as a matter all of whose other connections are dropped; a sort of secret game that can go on only if each of the parties has nothing to do, even on any *other* terms, with any one else.[5]

And Lawrence typically expands this to: "Marriage is the clue to human life, but there is no marriage apart from the wheeling sun and the nodding earth, from the straying of the planets and the magnificence of the fixed stars." [6]

Immediately we see the old directional split reestablished: James's circuit depends upon domestic ties and Lawrence's upon universal. But we also see again the qualitative sharing of their faith that the finest and most central morality and meaning in life come with the relational extensions of genuine love. No more than Lawrence is James rooting love in the life of business ethics. He obviously does not mean that love should know how to count money and appraise art objects. After all, in the case of Charlotte Stant and Kate Croy, the love that counts and selects fine gifts is insufficient. The money in Milly's legacy is as disinterested as her commitment to love. And though his terms seem tame beside those of Lawrence, James might have been playing with a more refined distinction between the merely "personal" marriage and the "blood" marriage with love ultimately absorbing learning. Kate, whose love certainly extends more into the practical world than Milly's, is tainted with the "personalism" which becomes the wedge of that ego separation that prevents "blood marriage" and marks the "villains" of Lawrence. It is this wedge that forces dissolution of relationship before marriage. And could we not also term the "magnificent" original relationship of Charlotte and the Prince on the one hand (which, despite a veneer of sophistication, is even more naive in its way than the early one of Maggie) and that of Maggie and her father (an open affair that seems wrongfully secret) counterfeit by virtue of their isolationism and their deliberate abstracting of love from the rest of life? Nothing is surer than that the isolation of love negates its true moral value. It is by overt influence that the relationship of Chad and Mme de Vionnet, just before its inevitable break-up, is "morally" consummated. If the love which Milly and Maggie earn and shed seems to be the love of the spiritual savior, a metaphysically hermetic love, we must remember that their gifts necessarily have effect and influence in the social situation.

James sees in D'Annunzio's work a "singular incessant *leak* in the effect of distinction so artfully and so copiously produced . . . by a positive element of the vulgar." [7] D'Annunzio appears as pornographic to James as Richardson and Charlotte Brontë seem to Lawrence. In the first author, since it is isolated from love and love from life, sex seems deceptively larger than life; in the second two, it is the other way around—the pornographic element inheres in the secret sublimation of sex. But in both, natural relationship has been perverted. D'Annunzio's projection of the sexual picture is false because its spatial usurpation is quantitative, while fine morality grows in time and is qualitative. James explains it this way: "The vulgarity into which he so incongruously drops is, I will not say the space he allots to love-affairs, but the weakness of his sense of 'values' in depicting them." [8] Lawrence had observed that "if sex is the starting point and the goal as well, then sex becomes like the bottomless pit, insatiable. It demands at last the departure into death, the only available beyond." [9] The effect is parallel to the end of love in the western world, that of Carmen and Anna Karenina, and it is rejected as too easy and fruitlessly tragic by James as well as Lawrence.

It is all the more evident now why James's strongest heroines, Isabel and Maggie, and even Milly for that matter, are so far from self-destruction, why Isabel does not go into the sex-death of Goodwood's arms but instead into the complexities of living and relating despite the threat of "death in life," why Maggie does not close life in the arms of the Prince but opens it by experiencing "pity and dread" in the face of an absolute. Death, which defies time, is amoral, but life demands the values formed by choice and judgment.

James worried about the bonds of English "convention" in the novel, but he recognized the worth of such ties for combating this danger of an unanchored passion and a sexuality which not only belittled theme but character as well.[10] The English novel led passion into life by way of the very doors which seem to shut out the natural life: tact and taste. These qualities prevented the vulgar disproportions of isolation and made possible a working morality.

James does not attack the problem of "isolationism" in the novel only from the moral point of view. His concern is aesthetic, too, a concern for the story as much as for theme. When he treated Mme Serão's novels he wrote:

> It is not in short at all the moral but the fable itself that in the exclusively sexual light breaks down and fails us. Love, at Naples and in Rome, as Madame Serão exhibits it, is simply unaccompanied with any interplay of our usual conditions—with affectation, with duration, with circumstances or consequences, with friends, enemies, husbands, wives, children, parents, interests, occupations, the manifestation of tastes.[11]

Repeatedly James comes back, whether talking of the sexual obsession in D'Annunzio or the mediocrity of passion in Flaubert, to his protest against the deadening of relationship by the reduction of a character's specifiicity and depth; this was the ultimate aesthetic and ethical immorality:

> Who are these people, we presently ask ourselves, who love indeed with fury—though for the most part with astonishing brevity— but who are so without any suggested situation in life that they can only strike us as loving for nothing and in the void, to no gain

of experience and no effect of a felt medium or a breathed air. We know them by nothing but their convulsions and spasms, and we feel once again that it is not the passion of hero and heroine that gives, that can ever give, the heroine and the hero interest, but that it is they themselves, with the ground they stand on and the objects enclosing them, who give interest to their passion. This element touches us just in proportion as we see it mixed with other things, with all the things with which it has to reckon and struggle.[12]

The very fury of these lovers' thrashing is symptomatic of *lost* spontaneity and *limited* capacity and binds them to a stringent fate. The lack of extension and freedom in character relationship simply meant, for James, that the novelist was not trusting his characters adequately; he was putting his thumb in the pan.

James and Lawrence seem to cooperate particularly in two criticisms on this subject. They are closer, often, when they treat perversions of love than when they positively adjust, each in his own way, the balance of the sexes. James's reading of Sand and Lawrence's of Hardy are basically both concerned with the corruption of the trust between author and character due to a persistent imbalance in feminine or masculine dominance. Sand prejudices the freedom of her women in relationship by thrusting upon them her own needs, drives, or compensations—they "never in the least do [anything] for themselves, themselves as the 'sex,' they do them altogether for men." [13] The wavering between selfishness and service in the battle of the sexes (so cerebrally displayed in *Elle et lui*) is most complexly treated by James in the relationship of Kate Croy and Merton Densher. The problem comes to a climax as Merton Densher asks Kate (as a pledge of love) to come to him in his rooms in Venice before leaving him to his trying task. He speaks, like a good James character, of standing on his feet, and says to Kate:

> I take from you what you give me, and I suppose that, to be consistent—to stand on my feet where I do stand at all—I ought to thank you. Only, you know, what you give me seems to me, more than anything else, the larger and larger size of my job. It seems to me more than anything else what you expect of me. It never seems to me, somehow, what I may expect of *you*. There's so much you *don't* give me.[14]

Once again it is the used party who reflects the methods of the user, as Densher exploits sex for its "bargaining power." The contest between the sexes, once the dove's wings cover Kate and Densher, ends in a sad imbalance and turns upon the word "surrender." The relationship *had* been for some time dynamic and Kate and Densher *had* been faithful to the *idea* of it; at least there *had* been honor. But, Milly is not John Crowe Ransom's social "equilibrist" dove that comes crying "Honor, Honor"; she is rather the relational dove that cries, "Respect, Respect." In Sand's novel, and in her life as well, James finds that there is a fatal lack of respect in relationship. Of the Musset-Sand confessions James writes:

> The lovers are naked in the market-place and perform for the benefit of society. The matter with them, to the perception of the stupefied spectator, is that they entertained for each other every feeling in life but the feeling of respect. What the absence of that article may do for the passion of hate is apparently nothing to what it may do for the passion of love.[15]

Elle et lui reveals, to James's view, so much of the maleness in Sand herself that it crushes it in her mate. This imposition has dire effects on the novel and seriously limits its freedom for developing the terms of relationship, and hence for the "new" morality:

> George Sand is too inveterately moral, too preoccupied with that need to do good which is in art often the enemy of doing well. . . . It is just possible indeed that the moral idea was the real mainspring of her course—I mean a sense of duty of avenging on the unscrupulous race of men their immemorial selfish success with the plastic race of women. Did she wish above all to turn the tables—to show how the sex that had always ground the other in the volitional mill was on occasion capable of being ground?[16]

For Lawrence explicitly and James implicitly "whole love between man and woman is sacred and profane together," a burning together and burning apart "into separate clarity of being."[17] This balance in love between the sacred and profane is a dynamic equilibrium that is constantly shifting. Maggie must learn this lesson. When she saw the Prince as an image of romance her relationship was as prejudiced as George Sand's, for the romantic vision is, of course, a moral imposition. Her innocent "use" of the Prince made Charlotte's use of *her* possible. But when she appreciates marriage as both sacred and profane, when she has exposed her innocence and her marriage to the risks of metamorphosis (though risks far less dangerous than those of the dream of lasting innocence) she earns the romance of her royalty. The Prince himself has important lessons to learn on the difference between sympathy and respect.

In *The Bostonians* James had seen in the peculiarly Sandian imbalance a social history of "the decline of the sentiment of sex." [18] We would expect to find the strongest Laurentian reference with this equation of personal frustration and historical decay that is at best a minor note in James.[19] In Lawrence's view, imposed and predetermined intellectual "personalism," which destroys the possibilities of relationship through the dogmatism of one personality and which forces a disequilibrium in the love relationship, affects more than just an aspect of American society; it is a "deep psychic disease of modern men and women, . . . the atrophied condition of the intuitive faculties." [20]

Lawrence's most "literary" support of James, as Lawrence spoke more and more through himself and James more and more through his characters, comes in his essay on Hardy, where Lawrence focuses his observations on the Wessex novels and on the central "struggle into love." [21] Because Hardy himself is full of splits that refuse to heal, the projected literary struggle is marked by frustration. His personal predilection is for the "aristocrat," but his needs force him in practice to side with the community and condemn the "aristocrat." [22] The struggle becomes pathetic because a weak "life-flow" prohibits the individual from full relationship, whether it be Hardy himself or Troy, Clym, Tess, Jude. Flesh is divided from spirit and condemned to a stereotyped villainy.[23] In addition, the male principle destroys the female principle in the individual and in his relationships with other individuals. The irreconciled splits in Hardy's characters between the female and male principle are explored extensively by Lawrence, and the exploration ranges from Angel who denies the female in himself to Alec who acknowledges only the female in himself.[24] Jude is Tess turned round about, but the halves of male and female are inevitably split asunder and Hardy's characters must relinquish potential life and connection. Further, there is in the Hardy character a drive to escape the responsibility of full individuality and then full relationship.[25] In the land of no exit, "Jude and Sue are damned, partly by their very being, but chiefly by their incapacity to accept the conditions of their own and each other's being." [26] Hardy's characters cannot stand together, because they cannot stand alone. As Lilly preaches to Aaron in *Aaron's*

Rod which is largely a study of the preparation of the separate individual for relationship:

> Everybody ought to stand by themselves, in the first place—men and women as well. They can come together, in the second place, if they like. But nothing is any good unless each one stands alone, intrinsically.[27]

This difficult balance is more extensively explored in the celebrated terms of *Fantasia of the Unconscious*. Both Lawrence's Hardy and James's Sand, in vastly different ways, abort the potentiality of their character relationships by covering them with "mental consciousness" instead of infusing them with "phallic consciousness." [28] In his defense of *Lady Chatterley*, Lawrence showed literally and symbolically what this imposition could mean in terms of relationship. "Personalism" and "mental consciousness" isolate and paralyze Clifford who has lost "all connection with his fellow men and women, except those of usage." Gilbert Osmond suffers from a similar paralysis. Mellors, having still "the warmth of a man" is, nevertheless, like the Hardy characters who only start with this potential of phallic consciousness, "being hunted down." [29] The intensity of the public reaction to the "new" morality of *Lady Chatterley* is symptomatic of the different natures of the Laurentian and Jamesian novelistic sensibility. Lawrence projects his concerns with explicit, prophetic, poetic force even at the expense of stopping the novel's dramatic flow. James's manner is rather sympathetic and dramatic. But the issues debated and defended join the two authors by this central concern: the morality of the novel builds itself upon the base of free relationship. If James does not physically paralyze his Cliffords or make his Mellorses gamekeepers, his concern for relational freedom in character allows him, in more subtle ways, to cut across the bondage of old moralities and authorial impositions and to place at the center of his greatest books the image of the new and necessary "virtuous attachment."

✎§ VI *Two Moralities:*
Dogma and Relationship

The taint of Epictetus is the taint of slavery.[1]

Henry James

There is no doubt that when James talked about the necessary freedom of the modern novel he was thinking of the climate that would allow the most significant representations of relationship. We have repeatedly noted that, for James, the fineness of relationship shaped the quality of morality. Since we are used to thinking of general systems of morality as determinants and preservers of honest relationships, it might seem that James puts the cart before the horse.

The construction of the relational novel entailed important distinctions between the old and the new morality. In James's eyes, the old morality oversimplified relationship to the point of dishonesty, and it is worthwhile examining the reaction to this dishonesty that led him to assert: "The taint of Epictetus is the taint of slavery." [2] It is in an essay on Epictetus that James makes his most profound and most prolonged inquiry into the traditional differences between the philosopher's morality and that of the novelist. He turns the tables on philosophical systems by claiming that stoicism which, many readers maintain, marks James's moral attitudes, is essentially unphilosophic:

> It simplifies human troubles by ignoring half of them. It is a wilful blindness, a constant begging of the question. It fosters apathy and paralyzes the sensibilities. It is through our sensibilities that we suffer, but it is through them, too, that we enjoy; and when, by a practical annihilation of the body, the soul is rendered inaccessible to pain, it is likewise rendered both inaccessible and incompetent to real pleasure,—to the pleasure of action; for the source of half its impressions, the medium of its constant expression, the condition of human reciprocity, has been destroyed.[3]

Here is a paralyzing doctrine, totally unsuitable for the novel of dynamic relationship, of "human reciprocity." With the adoption of this "philosophy" there could be no metamorphic testing for character. It is a system which concentrates so hard upon the self in the service of forgetting the self that it encourages the "personalism" which James hated as much as Lawrence, and which made true relationship impossible:

> The grand defect of the system is, that it discourages all responsibility to anything but one's own soul. There is a somewhat apocryphal anecdote of Epictetus having said to his master, Epaphroditus, as the latter was about to put his leg into the torture, "You will break my leg"; and, when in a few moments this result was accomplished, of his having so quietly added, "Did not I tell you so?" It should be easy to quote this anecdote as an example of great nobleness of soul. But, on reflection, we see that it reveals, for our modern point of view, an astounding moral degradation.[4]

He who pretends to react to only half of life with the "nobility" of exclusion must, in perspective, accept the status of the flat character:

> There is no doubt that, on its own ground, Pagan brutality was best refuted by such means as these. But it is equally certain that such means as these are possible only to spirits tainted by the evils which they deplore. It is against the experience of such evils that they react; but as long as the battle is fought on the old ground, the reactionists only half secure our sympathy. To future ages they have too much in common with their oppressors. It is only when the circle is broken, when the reaction is leavened by a wholly new element, that it seems to us to justify itself. The taint of Epictetus is the taint of slavery.[5]

It is but one step more to the condemnation of Christian saintliness and asceticism (to which Flaubert was attracted), as a stultifier of dramatic debate. James's rejection of such a position for literature is a theme of two of his earliest pieces of criticism, reviews of Mlle de Guérin's journal and letters. In the earlier review James writes:

> The singular unity of her genius, indeed, is such as almost to qualify her for this distinction [that of being a classic]. As her brother was all complexity, she was all simplicity. As he was all doubt, she was all faith. It seems to us that we shall place Mlle de Guérin on her proper footing, and obviate much possible mis-

conception, if we say that here was an essentially *finite* nature.

. . . .

It was not that she was without imagination; on the contrary, she unmistakably possessed it; but she possessed it in very small measure. Religion without imagination is piety; and such is Mlle. de Guérin's profound contentment. She was, indeed, in a certain sense, impatient of life, but with no stronger impatience than such as the church was able to allay.[6]

It is obvious that this is not the impatience of James's heroines, not the willingness to live in doubt, to harbor the kind of negative capability that was essential to the Jamesian drama. (Even Jane Austen was to be chided for giving us an "arrested spring.") [7] The medieval saint [8] practices the morality of exclusion, and a certain and final court of appeal necessarily releases the soul from the engagements in complexity that James saw as the very essence of life. Milly's saintliness is not a choice, but a deprivation. It is genuine tragedy.

The clash between an inherited, stringent, complacent, or petty moral view of the "old ground," of the unbroken circle, and the new and free morality of the relational novel, is the basis of an actual struggle between Mark Ambient and his wife for the life of a child as it is the basis of the symbolic struggle between Mme. de Vionnet and Mrs. Newsome for the life of a man. It is no accident that James makes Strether playfully allude to Chad's paganism (p. 148) and Maria Gostrey to Mrs. Newsome as a "moral swell" (p. 43). In the novels we have been focussing upon, the description of a static morality (Mrs. Newsome is really *sitting* all through *The Ambassadors*) does not challenge James until it forms a pole for a dramatic contest. Quentin Anderson pertinently reminds us:

> It is . . . important to note . . . that those critics whose preferences among the novels lie with *The Bostonians, The Europeans, Washington Square, What Maisie Knew,* and *The Awkward Age* are in my eyes ducking the problem of tradition as it affects James, since they are occupied with those of his works which are . . . open, depending as they do on a spectrum of moral judgments and presumptions about the social scene which the reader possesses before he begins to read.[9]

What a difference there is between the set patterns of American morality displayed in *The Europeans* and the morality of Isabel Archer as she goes wayfaring and warfaring from her Puritan grounds. A lack of humor, of imagination, of energy, the "painful" view of life, which mark Mr. Wentworth's establishment are not, surely, attributes of Isabel Archer. The difference is most obvious when Felix completes an analysis which Gertrude begins:

> They [the Wentworths] look at it [life] as a discipline. . . .
> Well, that's very good. But there is another way . . . to look at it as an opportunity. (p. 74)

From the static moral vision, James moves impatiently to the superficial. Despite an avowed admiration for Trollope, James writes testily of the novel *Can You Forgive Her:*

> There are few of Mr. Trollope's readers who will not resent being summoned to pass judgment on such a sin as the one here presented, to establish by precedent the criminality of the conscientious flutterings of an excellent young lady. . . . Since forgiveness was to be brought into the question, why did not Mr. Trollope show us an error that we might really forgive—an error that would move us to indignation? It is too much to be called upon to take cognizance in novels of sins against convention, of improprieties; we have enough of these in life. We can have charity and pity only for real sin and real misery. We trust to novels to maintain us in the practice of great indignations and great generosities.[10]

Without the breaking of the circle by relationship, a "new element," reaction and character remain trivial. Trollope's heroine has no real sin as Epictetus has no real virtue. The great sin for James was the sin against relationship, a natural extension of Hawthorne's old unpardonable sin. The souls of Isabel, Maggie, and Milly suffer this great indignation with the recognition of betrayal in others and in themselves, and then, through a deepening reaction, grow quietly and beautifully into a state of great generosity. But if the James novel moved in only one oversimplifying direction of exploiter and exploited, it would be in its own way stained with the taint of Epictetus. We have seen that the innocent also, even Milly, can exploit by their innocence and tempt into villainy. It is this counter-movement which deepens reaction.

As we have seen him do so often, James pits his novelistic preference for the "new morality" against the work of significant novelists. He underlines the weakening of Eliot's work in both form and content by her preaching of the old morality. Constantius says in the dialogue on *Daniel Deronda:*

In the manner of the book, throughout, there is something that one may call a want of tact. The epigraphs in verse are a want of tact; they are sometimes, I think, a trifle more pretentious when really pregnant; the importunity of the moral reflections is a want of tact; the very diffuseness is a want of tact. . . . She does not strike me as naturally a critic, less still as naturally a sceptic; her spontaneous part is to observe life and to feel it, to feel it with admirable depth. Contemplation, sympathy and faith—something like that, I should say, would have been her natural scale. If she had fallen upon an age of enthusiastic assent to old articles of faith, it seems to me possible that she would have had a more perfect, a more consistent and graceful development than she has actually had.[11]

She sometimes forced the moral idea over the moral drama, criticism over the novel: "Instead of feeling life itself, it is 'views' upon life that she tries to feel." [12] Of course, this is only one side of a dialogue, but it represents clearly an aspect of Eliot that bothered James considerably. Eliot's moral emphasis is ideological, and the novelist who projects the priority of relationship, who counts upon his characters to stand on their own feet, must avoid it.

The French have been good for the ailments of English modesty, but the "business . . . of the senses" is by no means "the only typical one" [13] as the basis for freeing us from the old morality, and we are still, with it, chained to a dogma of the flesh. We have seen how much flatter even this reaction is than Eliot's. English modesty has its advantages as well as disadvantages. For one thing, "whereas we like to be good, the French like to be better." This means that "we like to be moral, they to moralize," [14] and it is not difficult to judge which nature is healthier for the novel that James preferred. From one point of view Eliot's weakness touches that of the French. The novelist moralizes didactically only when morality is not allowed to grow dramatically in the novel itself. (This is not, often, true of Eliot.) The mere absence of explicit authorial moralizing does not guarantee a change in this effect: the distancing ironies of the naturalistic and Flaubertian attitudes force the reader to moralize rather than to share in the formation of moral values within the drama.

The French example can mock English modesty only at the price of belittling central consciousness. The less freedom and consciousness the novelist allows his character, the less modesty will the character need. But the sacrifice of consciousness, freedom, and hence modesty (elsewhere, the capacity for conduct) means the sacrifice of the moral to the moralizing, the sympathetic to the ironic mode:

> The Parisians profess, we believe, to have certain tendencies in common with the old Athenians; this unshrinking contemplation of our physical surfaces might be claimed as one of them. Practically, however, it gives one a very different impression from the large Greek taste for personal beauty; for the French type, being as meagre as the Greek was ample, has been filled out with the idea of "grace," which, by implying that the subject is conscious, makes modesty immediately desirable and the absence of it vicious.[15]

There is no loss greater to James than the loss of the deliberate repression of the moral imagination that fuses consciousness with drama, author with character. It is dulled by the total dependence on "the illimitable alchemy of art"[16] which the "art for art" cultists sponsor; it is dulled as well by the easy substitution of the sentimental interest for the relational. For the business of the moral imagination is the control and development of genuine drama. James takes Turgenev once again for his ally:

> The husband, the wife, and the lover—the wife, the husband and the woman loved—these are combinations in which modern fiction has been prolific; but M. Turgenieff's treatment renews the youth of the well-worn fable. He has found its moral interest, if we may take the distinction, deeper than its sentimental one; a pair of lovers accepting adversity seem to him more eloquent than a pair of lovers grasping at happiness.[17]

If James deplored the prejudice of ideology, sentimentality, art for art, and the obsession of physical surface, he was infuriated by the presence of oversimplified, faked and rigid moral principles to the exclusion of natural moral variety. Great indignations and great generosities grow and are qualified; they are not fabricated. The lack of this understanding is what he complained of in the Kingsleys:

> The main object of the novels of Mr. Charles Kingsley and his brother has seemed to us to be to give a strong impression of what they would call "human nobleness." Human nobleness, when we come across it in life, is a very fine thing; but it quite loses its flavor when it is made so cheap as it is made in these works. It is emphatically an occasional quality; it is not, and with all due respect for the stalwart Englishmen of Queen Elizabeth's time and eke of Queen Victoria's, it never was the prime element of human

life, nor were its headquarters at any time on the island of Great Britain. By saying it is an occasional quality, we simply mean that it is a great one, and is therefore manifested in great and exceptional moments. In the ordinary course of life it does not come into play; it is sufficiently represented by courage, modesty, industry. Let the novelist give us these virtues for what they are, and not for what no true lover of human nature would have them pretend to be, or else let him devise sublime opportunities, situations which really match the latent nobleness of the human soul.[18]

This kind of nobility is as reductive of genuine individuality and relationship as anything the naturalists could perpetrate. Writing of the "noble" school of fiction, James proclaims:

There is . . . in the human imagination a force which respects nothing but what is divine. In the muscular faith there is very little of the divine, because there is very little that is spiritual. For the same reason there is nothing but a spurious nobleness.[19]

While the Eliots, Kingsleys, and Maupassants suffered from the excess, oversimplification, or rejection of an old morality, the American novelist was faced with a different problem in his struggle towards the full use of the novel's potentiality. The "chilly and isolated sense of moral responsibility" which characterizes the New Englander, compensates for a lack of a traditional social standpoint and moral expectation. The continental citizen has this advantage:

That his standards are fixed by the general consent of the society in which he lives. A Frenchman, in this respect, is particularly happy and comfortable . . . his standards being the most definite in the world, the most easily and promptly appealed to, and the most identical with what happens to be the practice of the French genius itself. The Englishman is not quite so well off, but he is better off than his poor interrogative and tentative cousin beyond the seas.[20]

In a more personal appeal, James has his sad artist of "The Madonna of the Future" complain:

We're the disinherited of Art! We're condemned to be superficial! We're excluded from the magic circle! The soil of American perception is a poor little barren artificial deposit! Yes, we're wedded to imperfection! An American, to excel, has just ten times as much to learn as a European! We lack the deeper sense! We have neither taste nor tact nor force! How should we have them?

Our crude and garish climate, our silent past, our deafening present, the constant pressure about us of unlovely conditions, are as void of all that nourishes and prompts and inspires the artist as my sad heart is void of bitterness in saying so! We poor aspirants must live in perpetual exile.[21]

Our immediate impression is that we have heard this complaint in more celebrated circumstances, in the fine Hawthorne essay where James sympathizes with Hawthorne's own worries about writing in a country devoid of shadow and tradition.[22] (Actually, their complaints tend in different directions. Hawthorne went to Europe, in *The Marble Faun,* for symbols and pictures of sin to make life convincing. James went for a sophisticated society and tradition that had domesticated sin and uses art as a dangerous analogy to life.) The Boston of the past was a "ministry without opposition." [23] But the reader is well aware, by this time, of James's way of circling his views, of avoiding over-simplification in both his novels and criticism. From his earliest articles, particularly on the subject of America, his points were points of debate rather than opinion. Roderick Hudson, for example, took the very opposite tack from that of the artist Theobald:

It's a wretched business . . . this virtual quarrel of ours with our own country, this everlasting impatience that so many of us feel to get out of it. . . . This is an American day, an American landscape, an American atmosphere. It certainly has its merits, and some day when I'm shivering with ague in classic Italy I shall accuse myself of having slighted them.[24]

In an essay on Emerson, James actually found consolation in the lack of tradition:

I have hinted that the will, in the old New England society was a clue without a labyrinth; but it had its use, nevertheless, in helping the young talent to find its mould. There were few or none ready-made: tradition was certainly not so oppressive as might have been inferred from the fact that the air swarmed with reformers and improvers.[25]

But is there, James wondered, enough moral substance in the "American atmosphere" to allow the artist to dip below the surface of mere impressionism? The irony implicit in Roderick's own naiveté about the American scene, which actually mistrusts the depth of the American social soil, and the narrator's answer to the artist *"raté"* in "The Madonna of the Future" are James's warning to us not to despair. Theobald is not nourished by the false idealism that keeps him from America, but rather he dies turning it into a travesty of the real. The narrator observes with some impatience: "Nothing is so idle as to talk about our want of a nursing air, of a kindly soil, of opportunity, of inspiration, of the things that help. The only thing that helps is to do something fine." [26]

It is important to remember that James is interested in rescuing whatever there is of the American moral substance for the sake of creating his own; the moral elevation of relationship seemed a natural American response, and one that had not been exploited. When he deplores in his own day the "sinking of manners . . . which the democratization of the world brings with it" [27] or the "thinly-composed society" of Hawthorne's time he is really deploring the fact that the writer has difficulty finding himself "in any variety of intimacy of relations with any one or with anything." [28] Hawthorne's morality, potent and imaginative in itself, is the morality of romance, and romance alone, as we have seen, does not develop the Jamesian relationship. His romance, like the existentialist hero, carries the burden of too much freedom with it, and it enslaves itself to the rigidity of allegory in compensation. Its characters seek to fulfill a pre-established pattern of morality assigned to them, and the predictable picture that James's characters must turn from is inevitably painted. Hawthorne uses morality "as an imaginative tool"; it does not arise out of evolving relationship:

> The conscience, by no fault of its own, in every genuine offshoot of that sombre lineage, lay under the shadow of the sense of *sin*. This darkening cloud was no essential part of the nature of the individual; it stood fixed in the general moral heaven under which he grew up and looked at life. It projected from above, from outside, a black patch over his spirit, and it was for him to do what he could with the black patch.[29]

Hawthorne's great artistic feat, when he is successful, is the graceful transmutation of the black patch into the texture of his story. He can do this, ironically, precisely because his morality does not arise out of relationship, but is used from the beginning as a tool of artistic formation; for, as James observed, "Nothing is more curious and interesting than this almost exclusively *imported* character of the sense of sin in Hawthorne's mind; it seems to exist there merely for an artistic or literary purpose." [30] In a later essay (1897) he describes Hawthorne's situation like this:

> On the surface—the surface of the soul and the edge of tragedy—he preferred to remain. He lingered, to weave his web, in the thin exterior air. This is a partial expression of his characteristic habit of dipping, of diving just for sport, into the moral world without being in the least a moralist. He had none of the heat nor of the dogmatism of that character; none of the impertinence, as we feel he would almost have held it, of an intermeddling. He never intermeddled; he was divertedly and discreetly contemplative, pausing oftenest wherever, amid prosaic aspects, there seemed most of an appeal to a sense for subtleties. But of all cynics he was the brightest and kindest, and the subtleties he spun are mere silken threads for stringing polished beads. His collection of moral mysteries is the cabinet of a dilettante. [31]

Though this commentary is meant to be descriptive rather than severely critical, it delineates once again the studio of a painter of morality.

It is distance that gives the Hawthorne romance both its charm and its unfortunate static tendency. When Hawthorne extends his allegorical mechanisms such as the "A" in *The Scarlet Letter,* he thins the texture of the romance to "physical comedy" rather than enriching it with "moral tragedy." Naturally, he is at the same time moving farther and farther away from the possibilities of intense relationship. James astutely observed in the later essay that it is the reflected "picture" in the background rather than the active pursuit in the foreground that, ironically, vivifies *The Scarlet Letter,* and we can imagine that James intentionally aimed for a similar structural effect in *The Wings of the Dove:*

> Yet the main achievement of the book is not what is principally its subject—the picture of the relation of two men. They are too faintly—the husband in particular—though so fancifully figured. *The Scarlet Letter* lives, in spite of too many cold concetti—Hawthorne's general danger—by something noble and truthful in the image of the branded mother and the beautiful child. Strangely enough, this pair are almost wholly outside the action; yet they preserve and vivify the work. [32]

But it seems fair to speculate that James's preference for *The House of the Seven Gables* is based upon the vitality of a foreground that features attempts at communication, that holds its own against the dire imminence of the past, the complacent security of a picture.

It was because Hawthorne did not have a deep belief in the only "old" morality America had to offer, Puritanism, that he was able to use it as a picturesque temper. In this sense then, his romance could be said to emerge out of a reaction to an old morality, but he was, given his relation to it, confined to romance:

> The old Puritan moral sense, the consciousness of sin and hell, of the fearful nature of our responsibilities and the savage character of our Taskmaster—these things had been lodged in the mind of a man of Fancy, whose fancy had straightway begun to take liberties and play tricks with them—to judge them (Heaven forgive him!) from the poetic and aesthetic point of view, the point of view of entertainment and irony. This absence of conviction makes the difference. . . .[33]

Hawthorne condemns himself to the outer circle of morality, the rim of the picturesque, the rim from which, for all James's love and respect for his American Virgil, James would not free him. Hawthorne's picturesque, loosened from conviction, clings too tenaciously to allegory for James's sensibility:

> Hawthorne, in his metaphysical moods, is nothing if not allegorical, and allegory, to my sense, is quite one of the lighter exercises of the imagination . . . it is apt to spoil two good things—a story and a moral, a meaning and a form; and the taste for it is responsible for a large part of the forcible—feeble writing that has been inflicted upon the world. (p. 63)

All of these aesthetic consequences have great relevance to the relational novel. If the American author is condemned to a more and more rarified romance because of the lack of a complex, substantial, and living moral tradition, then the American character is condemned as well to the horror of too irresponsible a freedom. It is a cultural trait that the great Jamesian American heroines, Maggie, Isabel, Milly take to Europe in their vision of romance, of the moral picturesque; they are like Hawthorne, allegorists of the human soul (p. 66). But if the dogma of romance, born out of too much freedom in the library rooms of Albany houses, condemns temporarily to isolation, it also is the very great hope and leaven for personal wholeness and for the priority of relationship. The American heroine who comes from such freedom has the chance to create morality out of the holiness of the heart's affections. It is Maggie, after all, not the Prince, who shapes both the aesthetic and the ethical scope of her novel.

As James's own novelistic vision works to fuse romance and the real (a structural and psychological growth which takes physical root in the blending of America and Europe), his great heroines, by their growing understanding of the reality of human commitment, deepen the substance of the American novel. James had little patience with those who would cut off this potential through artistic or national timidities. This was the essence of his argument with Howells. The novel, of all forms, must use the freedom it so abundantly has access to: "if it perishes this will surely be by its fault—by its superficiality, in other words, or its timidity." [34]

From the standpoint of the necessary and genuine freedom, America then, despite its terrible vacancies, offers to the novelist and heroine a rich birthplace. To his English speaking brothers in general James gives this encouragement:

> Let us then leave this magnificent art of the novelist to itself and to its perfect freedom, in the faith that one example is as good as another, and that our fiction will always be decent enough if it be sufficiently general. Let us not be alarmed at this prodigy (though prodigies are alarming) of M. de Maupassant, who is at once so licentious and so impeccable, but gird ourselves up with the conviction that another point of view will yield another perfection. [35]

James asserts again and again: "The form of novel that is stupid on the general question of its freedom is the single form that may *a priori* be unhesitatingly pronounced wrong." [36] Naturally, warns James, "A community addicted to reflection and fond of ideas will try experiments with the 'story' that will be left untried in a community mainly devoted to travelling and shooting, to pushing trade and playing football. . . ." [37] But in a society grown habituated to literary timidity, the novelist above all can make the national heritage meaningful by deepening and renewing the treatment of "the great relation between men and women." [38] That is why James welcomes the influence of the feminine side, in the hope that we may see "the female elbow itself, kept in increasing activity by the plan of the pen, smash with final resonance the window all this time most superstitiously closed." [39]

Part of the window smashing can be done, James reflects, through the characters themselves. The novel cannot be free when morality is

imposed upon character rather than evolving from it. As the novel
loses force without a formative moral freedom, so does character.
James was aware that the allowance of liberty to one's subjects is not
an easy task. The temptations to escape the discomfort of flexibility
by the imposition of ethical assumption is strong in the English
novel. Both Thackerary and Eliot were guilty of it, among the masters. Why, for example, should Arthur Donnithorne be redeemed.

> Arthur Donnithorne was a superficial fellow, a person emphati-
> cally not to be moved by a shock of conscience into a really inter-
> esting and dignified attitude. . . . Why not see things in their
> nakedness? . . . Why not let passions and foibles play themselves
> out? [40]

Instead of love, respect, and freedom, Thackerary brought to Becky
a desire to "expose and desecrate." This lack of sympathy makes
Thackeray, in the eyes of James, a strong contrast to Balzac who *aime
sa Valérie*. Balzac has many flaws, but his great powers of sympathy
and saturation enabled him to experience a love of his characters,
"the joy in their communicated and exhibited movement, in their
standing on their own feet and going of themselves," [41] a talent that
to James was essential for the novelistic exploitation of freedom and
plasticity:

> How do we know given persons, for any purpose of demonstra-
> tion, unless we know their situation for themselves, unless we see
> it from their point of vision, that is from their point of pressing
> consciousness or sensation?—without our allowing for which there
> is no appreciation. Balzac loved his Valérie then as Thackeray did
> not love his Becky. . . . But his prompting was not to expose her;
> it could only be, on the contrary—intensely aware as he was of
> all the lengths she might go, and paternally, maternally alarmed
> about them—to cover her up and protect her, in the interest of her
> special genius and freedom. All his impulse was to *la faire valoir*,
> to give her all her value, just as Thackeray's attitude was the oppo-
> site one, a desire positively to expose and desecrate poor
> Becky. . . .[42]

To allow the fullness of a character's "special genius and freedom" to develop, the novelist must learn to avoid the easy lures of
doctrine, unmitigated irony, false nobility, or the moral picturesque.
The freedom which James demands involves an authorial sacrifice for
the sake of character. If relationship is to support both the compositional and ethical weight of the novel, then it must appear only to be

briefly born from the head of its father before leaving home. That James's own relationship to his characters is intimate and trusting is most engagingly seen when James teases us into an impression of shared composition. The second part of *The Golden Bowl*, for example, seems to be actually composed by Maggie. James writes in his preface to *The Golden Bowl*:

> The Princess, in fine, in addition to feeling everything she has to and to playing her part just in that proportion, duplicates, as it were, her value and becomes a compositional resource.[43]

The game of total trust is a serious game, and at his gayest, in *The Sacred Fount*, for example, James is illustrating an important aesthetic point. The two major knots of relationship which must be continually opened, probed, metamorphosed, are that between author and character, and character and character. If this activity is honest and interesting, the reader can take care of himself. In *The Sacred Fount*, James is exploring the delightful possibilities of aesthetic metamorphosis in authorial composition, while in *The Golden Bowl*, he is particularly concerned with the way in which character, once trusted, can assume compositional powers and open itself up to the risks and rewards of moral metamorphosis. No character was in this way ever loved so much by James as was Maggie, the last of his great heroines. Let us turn, then, to these two very different books, one a critical exercise in the composition of the relational novel, the other itself the greatest of James's relational novels.

ᴥ§ VII *The Sacred Fount: an Author in Search of His Characters*

I say these things after all with the sense, so founded on past experience, that, in closer quarters and the intimacy of composition, prenoted arrangements, proportions and relations, do most uncommonly insist on making themselves different by shifts and variations, always improving, which impose themselves as one goes and keep the door open always to something *more* right and *more* related.[1]

Henry James

"Good heavens, Madam!" we are forever on the point of exclaiming, "let the poor things speak for themselves. What? are you afraid they can't stand alone?"[2]

Henry James

The Sacred Fount has proved irresistible to modern critics of James. Article after article has appeared in the last few years attempting a definitive explication of this puzzling book. For one thing, of course, critically, *The Sacred Fount* had been, until recent years, the "least done" of James's fiction. From the first significant articles of Wilson Follett[3] which suggested that James was parodying himself in the narrator, to Dorothea Krook's chapter in her fine book,[4] the major argument stems from the decision concerning the reliability of the narrator.[5]

If we assume that the book is a kind of cautionary tale, a moral fable, that our interpretive emphasis must be placed upon philosophical problems like "What is the relationship of Life to Art, Reality to Appearance," then we must also assume that the narrator is incomplete, that he is "an image of the artist *"manqué*,"[6] and that he violated his own gifts by pushing aesthetic curiosity beyond his moral sensibility. This point of view gains support from similar structure and theme in *The Turn of the Screw* and *The Aspern Papers,* and I would not deny the relevance of this angle of vision.

Nevertheless, the exuberant humor, the confession from James himself that the work is a "small fantasticality . . . a consistent joke," [7] suggests the possibility of another interpretation. I think we must honor Blackmur's reservations concerning the application of the term "novel" to this book and proceed to label it, as accurately as we can, a comic dialogue. By analogy to James's own dialogue on *Daniel Deronda,* it might be termed a "Conversation."

The subject of James's "consistent joke" is the art of composing a novel, and it has an aesthetic, not an ethical emphasis, though the aesthetic subject in James is always deeply moral. The plan depends upon James's own notebook practice epitomized in the notes to *The Ivory Tower;* it is a critical preface in action. Let us suppose that the narrator is, in actuality, not another character but James the novelist, who, having conceived a sketch for a new novel, projects himself into a fantasy of relationship with his characters, only to find that they, in their independent spontaneity, worry his original concepts of them by flexing the muscles of their possibilities. The narrator-novelist, knowing that good writing depends upon the trying out of possibilities in relationship, accepts his mock defeat by his own protean characters with good grace, proclaiming that he is still master of method even though Mrs. Briss, at least, has achieved her own independent tone. In one of his more appealing confessions, he is aware of the difficulty of keeping control of tones, of exercising sympathetic imagination in the face of created characters in the act of creation:

> These things—the way other people could feel about each other, the power not one's self, in the given instance, that made for passion—were of course at best the mystery of mysteries; still, there were cases in which fancy, sounding the depths or the shallows, could at least drop the lead. (p. 17)

How well James understood the depths and shallows allowed to his character relationships, and how careful actually he was in their control, is revealed in the notes to *The Ivory Tower* when he is probing the proper tones between Horton and Cissy:

> There are depths within depths between them—and I think I understand what I mean if I say there are also shallows beside shallows. They give each other rope and yet at the same time remain tied; that for the moment is a sufficient formula—once I keep the case lucid as to what their tie is. (p. 303)

What finally gives the novelist-narrator his most significant superiority over Mrs. Briss is his refusal, and her acceptance, of a limitation of consciousness in relationship only to the shallows. It is a mistake to agree with Mrs. Briss that the narrator is crazy, or with Ford Obert that he is a busy-body. James is having his own joke, granting to his characters a few extra drops of consciousness from the sacred fount (not so much Life or Art as the novelist himself) and, thereby, giving them the temporary privilege of judging him. The frequent compliments which the narrator addresses to his intellect, his instinct, his ingenuity, far from separating him from James himself, link him to the James of the notebooks, the James revelling in the exaggerated zest of composition. When critics complain that the narrator twists and turns hints and looks into words they are implying that a novelist has no right to fix the bounds of situation. No, the narrator is not a mad egotist—he is an elated novelist thoroughly enjoying the game of sharing composition with his more conscious characters.

The novelist does not accept authorial help from his less conscious characters. Of the dull Lady John he writes:

> She read all things, Lady John, heaven knows, in the light of the universal possibility of a "relation"; but most of the relations that she had up her sleeve could thrust themselves into my theory only to find themselves, the next minute, eliminated. They were of alien substance—insoluble in the whole. (p. 186)

In a later, more serious work, *The Golden Bowl*, James shares his game with Mrs. Assingham. It is significant that Ford Obert, Mrs. Briss, and Mrs. Assingham all, in spite of their perception, stop short of completion in the game. Literally, it is impossible, of course, for a character in a book to compete in composition with the author who sees the game to its end. The novelist has, after all, ultimate control, no matter how much freedom he grants his characters. But the case of Ford Obert tells us more.

In a crucial interview with Obert, the artist, whom James, perhaps, envisages as narrator of his novel, makes some fine observations on the distinction between the painter who fixes the grimace and the smile (as Obert fixed Mrs. Server's face in a portrait) and the novelist who must expose his fixed laws to assault by the flux of new possibilities of relationship. The narrator remarks:

I forbore—as I have hinted, to show all I saw, but it was lawfully open to me to judge of what other people did; and I had had before dinner my little proof that, on occasion, Obert could see as much as most. Yet I said nothing more to him for the present about Mrs. Server. The Brissendens were new to him, and his experience of every sort of facial accident, of human sign, made him just the touchstone I wanted. Nothing, naturally, was easier than to turn him on the question of the fair and the foul, type and character, weal and woe, among our fellow-visitors; so that my mention of the air of disparity in the couple I have just named came in its order and produced its effect. This effect was that of my seeing—which was all I required—that if the disparity was marked for him this expert observer could yet read it quite the wrong way. (p. 28)

The painter, without the *données* of the novelistic formula, might interpret literature in terms of art and hinder the flow of relationship. The narrator, it must always be assumed, is not made of the same stuff as the rest of the party—he is substance, his characters are yet shadows; he is life lending itself to art, while they are art trying to come to life. Obert is not finally a judge, but a touchstone. The narrator then presents to Obert his law, his "torch of analogy," from the sacred fount. Mr. Brissenden has sacrificed his youth and beauty to his older wife.

But with the advent of the crucial metaphor of the fount, James shows us that his narrator is the novelist in the act of composition, trying out upon his most perceptive character his law of compositional relationship before he can develop his law of moral relationship. (The extremism of the suggested subject matter, the vampire relationship between character and character, indicates James's preoccupation with the fantasy of testing novelistic construction.) The novelist himself must be sure to apportion the shares of consciousness and freedom among his characters in such a ratio that life will be afforded to all of them: "But the sacred fount is like the greedy man's description of the turkey as an 'awkward' dinner dish. It may be sometimes too much for a single share, but it's not enough to go round" (p. 29). Obert then understands that if the novelist is not careful, Mr. Briss might "die of the business" (p. 30), be drained of life not only by his wife but by the novelist himself. "How you polish them off!" he significantly exclaims, and the narrator answers: "I only talk . . . as you paint; not a bit worse! But one must indeed wonder . . . how the poor wretches feel" (p. 30).

It is the task of understanding the tones he himself has created which ultimately faces the novelist, and the mock failure of this effort produces a charming ending for the book. But the narrator is never seriously defeated. It is he, as the novelist whose major law is the law of flux and possibility in relationship, who finally moves away from Obert and Mrs. Briss, not the opposite movement which appears on the surface. Obert and Mrs. Briss, each in his way, are willing to expose and fix, even to the point of lying, to limit the dimensions of consciousness. It is the narrator, the "crazy busybody," who ironically protects his characters from being fixed. For the sake of freedom in the play of art, he even allows Mrs. Briss comically to run away with her own tone.

James has his fun with the less active members of his cast as well. His initial descriptions of the new (or newly conceived) Long masterfully reveal the variety in relationship not only between character and character, but between character and author:

> And the great thing was that if his eminence was now so perfectly graced he yet knew less than any of us what was the matter with him. He was unconscious of how he had "come out"—which was exactly what sharpened my wonder. Lady John, on her side, was thoroughly conscious, and I had a fancy that she looked to me to measure how far *I* was. I cared, naturally, not in the least what she guessed; her interest for me was all in the operation of her influence. I am afraid I watched to catch it in the act—watched her with a curiosity of which she might well have become aware. (p. 16)

The problem of the degree of consciousness granted by novelist and exercised by character in the range of object to subject, "fool" to "free spirit" is most extensively examined in the prefaces to *The Princess Casamassima, The Portrait of a Lady,* and *The Spoils of Poynton.* It is also, as Blackmur has hinted, of primary importance to *The Sacred Fount.* In fact, the climax of the book depends upon the battle Mrs. Briss and the narrator wage for the control of consciousness. As soon as he sees Mrs. Briss and Long together, the narrator wonders uneasily whether or not he can control the degree of consciousness granted them:

> The mind of man . . . doubtless didn't know from one minute to the other, under the appeal of phantasmagoric life, what it would profitably be at. It had struck me a few seconds before as vulgarly gross in Lady John that she was curious, or conscious, of so small

a part; in spite of which I was already secretly wincing at the hint that these others had begun to find themselves less in the dark and perhaps even directly to exchange their glimmerings.

My personal privilege, on the basis of the full consciousness, had become, on the spot, in the turn of an eye, more than questionable, and I was really quite scared at the chance of having to face—or having to see *them* face—another recognition. (p. 183)

It is at this point that the novelist asks the crucial question about his strong characters. Perhaps they are right to battle him *against* the enlargement of consciousness and hence *for* their privacy:

> What did this alarm imply but the complete reversal of my estimate of the value of perception? Mrs. Brissenden and Long had been hitherto magnificently without it, and I was responsible perhaps for having, in a mood practically much stupider than the stupidest of theirs, put them gratuitously and helplessly *on* it. To be without it was the most consistent, the most successful, because the most amiable form of selfishness; and why should people bright and insolent in their prior state, people in whom this state was to have been respected as a surface without a scratch is respected, be made to begin to vibrate, to crack and split, from within? (pp. 183-184)

It is the same question James might have asked himself later about the tortures of Maggie Verver. At the end of the book, in his great scene with Mrs. Briss, the narrator again admits to a scruple. He admits to the confession that "as it was I who had arrested, who had spoiled their [Long's and Mrs. Briss's] unconsciousness, so it was natural they should fight against me for a possible life in the state I had given them instead" (p. 295). The narrator may present scruples, but he knows that to leave his characters in this state of unconsciousness would be to substitute picturesqueness for dynamics, to make a portrait of a novel.

The preface to James's *The Portrait of a Lady* contains a strikingly parallel image to the picture we see at the beginning of *The Sacred Fount* when the novelist and two of his more important characters board the train to Newmarch. James is, while talking of Isabel, consistently one of his favorite "vessels" of consciousness, advocating a trust in one's characters, a trust in their relationships, a trust in the ability of those relationships to work themselves out. He says of his characters: "They were like the group of attendants and entertainers who come down by train when people in the country give a party; they represented the contract for carrying the party on." [8] The narrator of *The Sacred Fount* says at one point to his co-observer Mrs. Briss: "We're like the messengers and heralds in the tale of Cinderella, and I protest, I assure you, against any sacrifice of our denouement. We've still the glass shoe to fit" (p. 260). It is Mrs. Briss, not the narrator, who ultimately breaks the contract for "carrying the party on," the contract of mutual revelation of relationships. The narrator is secretly more than a messenger in his own game of metamorphosis from pumpkins to fairy coaches; he is, of course, the fairy godfather, exercising, for the sake of exploration, his permissive will.

It is significant that the narrator takes pleasure in his Cinderella metaphor, but Mrs. Briss is only confused by it. What is involved here is the great sacrifice the artist has to make for the sake of his art, and this sacrifice is reflected by his being deserted (on the levels of language as well as of plot) by his own characters as they flee from the responsibility of the larger vision. "What, artistically, would you do with it?" (p. 313) the narrator asks of Mrs. Briss who has objected to his manipulation of relationship. But this is not a question Mrs. Briss cares to concern herself with. As the narrator himself has mournfully reflected: "And I could only say to myself that this was the price—the price of the secret success, the lonely liberty and the intellectual joy" (p. 296). The James obsession with featuring the sensitive hero, heroine, or artist on whom the door of life is shut (Hyacinth, Strether, Milly) is here turned upon James himself. With the sad awareness of the price of joy, James writes in the notes to *The Ivory Tower:*

> I say these things after all with the sense, so founded on past experience, that, in closer quarters and the intimacy of composition, prenoted arrangements, proportions and relations, do most uncommonly insist on making themselves different by shifts and variations, always improving, which impose themselves as one goes and keep the door open always to something *more* right and *more* related. It is subject to that constant possibility, all the while, that one does pre-note and tentatively sketch; a fact so constantly before one as to make too idle any waste of words on it. At the same time I do absolutely and utterly want to stick, even to the very depth, to the *general* distribution here imagined as I have groped on; and I am at least now taking a certain rightness and conclusiveness of parts and items for granted until the intimate tussle, as I say, happens, if it does happen, to dislocate or modify them. . . . Variety, variety—I want to go in for that for all the possibilities of my case may be worth. . . .(pp. 350-351)

Is this not really what the narrator of *The Sacred Fount* holds as his compositional principle from the time he willingly goes with his characters, not to a Middlemarch of compromise, a village in which relationship is tied to social standards of fixed morality, but to a Newmarch where the possibilities of relationship are the possibilities of morality?

The privilege of self-conscious joy in his own composition makes the narrator at least as much a true prototype of James as of his fictional composers. James's notes to *The Ivory Tower* are filled with exclamations of the joy of composing, of composing by Laws, and of composing characters who exert their freedom by these Laws:

> By the blest operation this time of my Dramatic principle, my law of successive Aspects, each treated from its own centre, as, though with qualifications, The Awkward Age, I have the great help of flexibility and variety; my persons in turn, or at least the three or four foremost, having control, as it were, of the Act and Aspect, and so making it *his* or making it *hers*. (p. 276)

What pride James, like the narrator, takes in his patterns:

> This is exactly what I want, the tight packing *and* the beautifully audible cracking; the most magnificent masterfully little vivid economy, with a beauty of its own equal to the beauty of the donnée itself, that ever was. (p. 278)

Snatches like this are not uncommon as James searches to fit scene to conception: "But in fine—With which I cry Eureka, eureka; I have found what I want for Rosanna's connection, though it will have to make Rosanna a little older than Gray . . ." (p. 281), or "I seem to want something like his having consented to be 'put up' by her to the idea of offering Cissy something very handsome by way of a 'kind' tribute to her mingled poverty and charm—jolly, jolly, I think I've exactly got it!" (p. 327).

In the face of a particularly great challenge in proportioning of parts, James cheers himself up: "But why not? Who's afraid? and what has the very essence of my design been but the most magnificent packed and calculated closeness?" (p. 347). The point to be made here is that this attitude of the novelist in the face of his laws of composition is clearly the same which animates the narrator of *The Sacred Fount*. It comes out strongly during his interview with Mrs. Server ("I was morally confident and intellectually triumphant . . .";

"I was dazzled by my opportunity . . .") (p. 142), but most clearly in a late talk with Mrs. Briss. At this point (ch. 12), the narrator, using terms from James's own literary criticism, is so pleased by the "accumulations of lucidity" that he is sure they "defy all leakage" (p. 256). He recognizes Mrs. Briss's desertion of the "contract" and sees himself trying to catch for her the lost thread, actually "stooping to the carpet for it and putting it back in her hand" (p. 258). But James knows that only the author sees completely the "figure in the carpet." Mrs. Briss wants from now on to use her privileges of freedom of tone, at least, and to fix her consciousness, but the narrator is aware that if he surrenders to fixity, the art of the novel is destroyed.

So willing is the novelist to allow his characters all the freedom possible for the sake of rich plot and theme that he involves himself in being deceived as well as in deceiving. The atmosphere of fairyland (especially strong in Chapter VIII) pervades the book and confines the working out of relationships to the land of characters. (This process extends suggestively to *The Golden Bowl*.) There is no immediate retreat for the narrator into life once he has willingly entered the palace of art, and by entering the palace of his characters, he temporarily and playfully suspends his powers of omniscience. It is clear from the beginning that Mrs. Server and Mrs. Briss are protecting truths from his grasp. Mrs. Briss is trying to sabotage the creator's law all the way to prevent the enlargement of consciousness which would reveal her as cruel in her knowledge of sacrifice, the sacrifice of her husband demanded by the narrator's law of victor and victim in the draining of beauty, youth, and wit. The novelist struggles to keep her as his ficelle-observer in his novel. For Mrs. Server, the role of possible heroine is reserved and the novelist, who fancies at one point that he is in love with her, attempts to protect her from "disintegration" (p. 167) in the game of sacrifice. It is this constant deception which lends to the book its air of detective story and to the narrator at times the personality of a Poe in search of a solution.

But the real difference between the narrator and his characters emerges vividly in Chapter IX. The characters are sitting around the dinner table and the narrator feels that there is a collective warning "not to yield further to my idle habit of reading into mere human things an interest so much deeper than mere human things were in general prepared to supply" (p. 156). What the characters do not realize is that relationship itself adds to the amount of substance each participant has to give. At one point the narrator had mused on his analogies:

> It put before me the question of whether, in these strange relations that I believed I had thus got my glimpse of, the action of the person "sacrificed" mightn't be quite out of proportion to the resources of that person. It was as if these elements might really multiply in the transfer made of them; as if the borrower practically found himself—or herself—in possession of a greater sum than the known property of the creditor. (p. 53)

In Chapter IX, the narrator has wandered into a scene in which each character granted life by him is intent upon developing himself in his own private relationships. But merely working by themselves, without the novelist's power of transmuting vision, without his gift of full consciousness, they present only very flat lives. It is, after all, the *way* in which the author sees his characters that gives them the life they pretend to have created themselves. The narrator meditates:

> This especial hour, at Newmarch, had always a splendour that asked little of interpretation, that even carried itself, with an amiable arrogance, as indifferent to what the imagination could do for it. I think the imagination, in those halls of art and fortune, was almost inevitably accounted a poor matter; the whole place and its participants abounded so in pleasantness and picture, in all the felicities, for every sense, taken for granted there by the very basis of life, that even the sense most finely poetic, aspiring to extract the moral, could scarce have helped feeling itself treated to something of the snub that affects—when it does affect—the uninvited reporter in whose face a door is closed. . . . We existed, all of us together, to be handsome and happy, to be really what we looked. . . . Hadn't everyone my eyes could at present take in a fixed expressiveness? (pp. 156-157)

We have noted that one of James's most consistent themes in his criticism and novels is that the picturesque of relationship, as contrasted to the dynamic flux of relationship, is immoral. He defends *Daniel Deronda,* we remember, by defending its amount of felt life: "In life without art you can find your account; but art without life is a poor affair." [9] Against his characters' inclination to freeze their relationships, to remain picturesque, to limit consciousness, to prefer an Obert portrait to a James novel, the narrator as novelist stands as the defender of moral potentialities in relationship. It is the infusion of moral sense into the picturesqueness of the scene which makes possible the creative vision of a novel. We need only recall James's own great defense of "the posted presence of the watcher" in his preface to *The Portrait of a Lady* to remember to defend the narrator of *The Sacred Fount:*

> The house of fiction has in short not one window, but a million— a number of possible windows not to be reckoned, rather; every one of which has been pierced, or is still pierceable, in its vast front, by the need of the individual vision and by the pressure of the individual will. . . . The spreading field, the human scene, is the "choice of subject"; the pierced aperture, either broad or balconied or slit-like and low-browed, is the "literary-form"; but they are, singly or together, as nothing without the posted presence of the watcher—without, in other words, the consciousness of the artist. Tell me what the artist is, and I will tell you of what he has *been* conscious. Thereby I shall express to you at once his boundless freedom and his "moral" reference.[10]

Though his characters in Newmarch's palace of art may lose interest in their author, we can be sure that the author will never give up on his characters.

⚜ VIII *The Metamorphic Movement in The Golden Bowl*

Near the royal castle there was a great dark wood, and in the wood under an old linden-tree was a well; and when the day was hot, the King's daughter used to go forth into the wood and sit by the brink of the cool well, and if the time seemed long, she would take out a golden ball and throw it up and catch it again, and this was her favourite pastime. Now it happened one day that the golden ball, instead of falling back into the maiden's little hand which had sent it aloft, dropped to the ground near the edge of the well and rolled in. The King's daughter followed it with her eyes as it sank, but the well was deep, so deep that the bottom could not be seen. Then she began to weep, and she wept and wept as if she could never be comforted. And in the midst of her weeping she heard a voice saying to her, "What ails thee, King's daughter? Thy tears would melt a heart of stone."

And when she looked up to see where the voice came from, there was nothing but a frog stretching his thick ugly head out of the water. "Oh, it is you, old waddler?" she said. "I weep because my golden ball has fallen into the well."

"The Frog Prince," Grimm's Fairy Tales

Eve:

> But now lead on;
> In me is no delay; with thee to go,
> Is to stay here; without thee here to stay,
> Is to go hence unwilling; thou to me
> Art all things under Heaven, all places thou,
> Who for my wilful crime art banished hence.

Paradise Lost, XII, 614-619.

It is not really paradoxical that James, whom most critics call a psychological realist, should have been consistently impelled towards the fairy-tale structure. Nowhere is this attraction more apparent than in *The Golden Bowl*. The young Princess must win her Prince who, under an evil spell, has become a Frog. She must conquer him by love and knowledge, enter the carriage with her Frog-Prince, transformed once more back to his old self, and ride away from the realm of the Father-King. The means of living, the furniture of existence, are more than ever simplified. But at the center of the fairy-tale, as James tells it, squats the Satanic toad of Eden who demands, by his very presence, growth of consciousness and conscience in the face of a new reality. A Prince does not, in the world of James, become a husband when a frog is hurled petulantly against the wall. Marriage must be earned in pain, and Eve the redeemer must learn to leave the first Eden of childhood so that she can enter the second, in which new burdens of knowledge and responsibility are eased by new depths of relationship. In the domain of *The Golden Bowl*, Henry James for once allows marriage to carry us where we would like to go, into the world of romance that spins on the "beautiful circuit and subterfuge of our thought and our desire," but we ride heavily on real wheels, wheels that stand for "the things we cannot possibly not know."

Whatever complex thematic culminations James's last great books may contain, and they are many, *The Golden Bowl* is essentially the purest novel of relationship in the James canon. The fairy façade, instead of overlaying the serious moral substance of human relationship, emphasizes it by freeing the novel from its usual fixed social and historical attachments and concerns. Though this last novel is the boldest in its use of the magic world, we have seen numerous similar allusions and patterns already in *The Portrait, The Ambassadors,* and *The Wings of the Dove* with their Princes and Prosperos, Princesses and Mirandas. Fairyland's deceptive offers of magic, its gratuitous gifts, always lead us back to the major message that beauty, strength, and depth of relationship depend upon the courage to take the ethical risks of changing consciousness, and a charmed world leads there all the more easily because the scenes and images through which its roads pass, themselves submit to the aesthetic law of metamorphosis. What Maggie learns, and then what she shows us, is a moral truth about marriage as deep as that of Isabel's, and we ought not to allow ourselves to be prejudiced by the depth of Isabel's suffering as she turns back to the institution of marriage in a seemingly hopeless attempt to infuse ritual with relationship, or by Milly's tragic state where even death insists upon keeping her life only ritual. Maggie, of all James's heroines, comes closest ultimately to the happiness of romance, but she has had to endure real trials and a real sacrifice in order to arrive.

It is Maggie who, with the advent of full consciousness and hence pain, assumes the risks of working in the metamorphic state, the risks of composition, and with her strengthening vision, guides not only souls but scenes and images to marriage. While in Part One Fanny Assingham composes loudly and intelligently, making sure that Colonel Assingham (and the rest of us) can hear and understand, in Part Two we are led, with the surging lift in image and conscience, into deeper chambers of involvement, and a conscious Maggie goes morally deeper than the socially thorough Fanny. Because Maggie plans, not for an audience but for her Prince and her father, whose involved sensibilities contrast with the Colonel's "non-amphibious" state, she must take care not to injure the quality of relationship. She must work quietly and without help. She must pay a price for her painful control, for her almost religious consistency. As the metamorphic priestess-princess she carries her hard earned and newly reformed golden bowl just before her last great sacrificial scene with Charlotte:

> Just now she was carrying in her weak, stiffened hand a glass filled to the brim, as to which she had recorded a vow that no drop should overflow. She feared the very breath of a better wisdom, the jostle of the higher light, of heavenly help itself; and, in addition, however that might be, she drew breath this afternoon, as never yet, in an element heavy to oppression.[1]

Maggie, of course, can know only part of the larger authorial reference which makes this pictured gesture a climax of metamorphic process. We understand, as she cannot, that her willingness to risk metamorphosis, a risk which includes the use of deliberate lies and illusive appearances for the sake of reality, even at times "not by a hair's breadth, deflecting into truth" (II, 250-251), contrasts with the uneasy bravado of both the Prince and Charlotte on the great Matcham afternoon. Charlotte, thinking of the golden bowl, remonstrates with the Prince: " 'Don't you think too much of 'cracks,' and aren't you too afraid of them? I risk the cracks. . . .' " And the

Prince answers: " 'Risk them as much as you like for yourself, but don't risk them for me' " (I, 359-360). Before that, the Prince had felt the day "like a great gold cup that we must somehow drain together." Eventually, by attaining full consciousness, Maggie herself may guide the Prince, together with Charlotte and the golden bowl, to the climax of her metamorphic stand. With the changing bowl, she projects to the end the vivid cage imagery with which she has surrounded the doomed Charlotte. She carefully brings the two long tracings together as she imagines Charlotte's plea from behind a confining glass:

> "You don't know what it is to have been loved and broken with. You haven't been broken with, because in *your* relation what can there have been, worth speaking of, to break? Ours was everything a relation could be, filled to the brim with the wine of consciousness; and if it was to have no meaning, no better meaning than that such a creature as you could breathe upon it, at your hour, for blight, why was I myself dealt with all for deception? Why condemned after a couple of short years to find the golden flame—oh, the golden flame!—a mere handful of black ashes?" (II, 329-330)

Of course, Charlotte cannot know how Maggie, applying her magic on character and image, has made her own golden fire rise like the phoenix from Charlotte's ashes. It is in the second part of *The Golden Bowl,* in which Maggie controls and guides with growing consciousness and courage the readjusted proportions of the enlarged family, that metamorphosis of major image is pressed into service for the larger moral ends of life, ends which must be nourished by the fairy, the religious, and the real. It is here that the fairy godmother, the priestess, and the woman are one.

Marriage compels the larger scene as well as the intimate image, to submit to the metamorphic process. Gardens must be revisited and carriage rides retaken before the right human balance is established. Maggie must revisit in order to see Eden changing, and she must travel until the magic carriage holds the proper relationship. (Though James took over the structure of revisited scene from Flaubert, he used it for almost diametrically opposed purposes. Isabel's revisiting of Gardencourt, Strether's of Chad's balcony, mark definitive change and development, while, in Flaubert, a comparison of carriage rides to Paris or Rouen, like the passage of objects from one house to the other and the blending of one woman into another, are all meant to show us how little has really changed or been educated.)

The whole structure stands upon both God and the fairy godmother, upon Eden and the Carriage. The finally projected voyage of Charlotte and Adam to the New World, with all its potential of art and science, is truly banishment from the second Eden of Maggie's marriage. Maggie's mind, flourishing in her great second part, plays with poetic and dramatic necessity upon scenes of garden and voyage. Her visions are rooted in a crucial garden interview with her father, Adam, where he pictures, in terms suggestive of godlike royalty, the danger of the original Edenic state of King and Princess as a "selfish prosperity":

> "That's the only take-off, that it has made us perhaps lazy, a wee bit languid—lying like gods together, all careless of mankind." . . . "Well, I mean too . . . that we haven't, no doubt, enough, the sense of difficulty." "Enough? Enough for what?" "Enough not to be selfish." (II, 90-91)

Adam Verver goes on daringly to suggest that there might even be a kind of immorality in their happiness. Becoming, like Maggie, conscious of new problems of relationship, he can ask his daughter:

> "You think then you could now risk Fawns?"
> "Risk it?"
> "Well, morally—from the point of view I was talking of; that of our sinking deeper into sloth." (II, 94)

Maggie is face to face with the necessity of taking moral and aesthetic risk in the metamorphic state, and she is aware that only by passing through and ordering such a state can she become the real Princess. Later, we see how Maggie has accepted this challenge as she both submits to and controls a garden scene which, according to the aesthetic and ethic of metamorphosis, reflects and refines an earlier one:

> It was positively as if, in short, the inward felicity of their being once more, perhaps only for half an hour, simply daughter and father had glimmered out for them, and they had picked up the pretext that would make it easiest. They were husband and wife— oh, so immensely!—as regards other persons; but after they had dropped again on their old bench, conscious that the party on the terrace, augmented, as in the past, by neighbours, would do beautifully without them, it was wonderfully like their having got together into some boat and paddled off from the shore where

husbands and wives, luxuriant complications, made the air too tropical. (II, 254-255)

She is tempted to sail off to that first, incest tainted, Byzantium. But, as so often in the major James (in *The Ambassadors* and "The Beast in the Jungle" both literally and figuratively), the boat trip, the shoving off from shore, represents the deepest, most energetic, and fruitful engagement, and Maggie will not be lured by her father's phantom sail. Once she recognizes the changes that have separated the two garden scenes, she is at most willing to accept the present moment only as a game, to play with the unmarried ease of her first paradise; "Well, then, that other sweet evening was what the present sweet evening would resemble; with the quite calculable effect of an exquisite inward refreshment" (II, 255). The climactic garden containing Charlotte and Maggie offers, like all magical gardens from a distance, the temptation of sloth, the easy avoidance of engagement. Maggie is, like Milly, and like Isabel, tempted "never to go down" when she sees the doomed Charlotte wandering in the garden at Fawns. She looks down from her "perched position" as if from some "castle-tower mounted on a rock." The noon garden has changed from former Edens: "The miles of shade looked hot, the banks of flowers looked dim; the peacocks on the balustrades let their tails hang limp and the smaller birds lurked among the leaves" (II, 306). But she knows she must descend because "the act of sitting still had become impossible" (II, 307).

The economical observer, involved in her own drama, who sees metamorphosis in scene, must also, of course, make the scene count for something in the rebirth of spirit. As she sees the scene then, Maggie meditates:

> The resemblance had not been present to her on first coming out into the hot, still brightness of the Sunday afternoon . . . but within sight of Charlotte, seated far away, very much where she had expected to find her, the Princess fell to wondering if her friend wouldn't be affected quite as she herself had been, that night on the terrace, under Mrs. Verver's perceptive pursuit. The relation, to-day, had turned itself round; Charlotte was seeing her come, through patches of lingering noon, quite as she had watched Charlotte menace her through the starless dark; and there was a moment, that of her waiting a little as they thus met across the distance, when the interval was bridged by a recognition not less soundless, and to all appearance not less charged with strange

meanings, than that of the other occasion. The point, however, was that they had changed places. . . . (II, 296)

This is our clearest perception of Maggie's assumption of the metamorphic process. Maggie's identifications seem like apt wish-fulfillments, the "doomed" Charlotte with the doomed Ariadne "roaming the lone seastrand" or Io "goaded by the gadfly," women who lived in a mythical world where transmutation was the magic of easy punishment or capture. But Maggie sees herself as "some far-off harassed heroine" (II, 307), and her role, because she is living it as well as observing it, has no precedent and is untouched by magic.

Images of Edenic light and flowers emerging from the night usher in the new moral dawning for Maggie. She has had to accustom herself to the role of "mistress of shades" (II, 142) before she can stand the glare of the garden at noon. After the Matcham affair, when Maggie's crucial meditation has exposed the already changing proportions of relationship, James writes with moving formality: "It was in the mitigated midnight of these approximations that she had made out the promise of her dawn" (II, 43). Ultimately she sees the Prince emerging from his silent purgatory full of something of the same promise granted to *him* by one of Maggie's last visions. Maggie lends beauty to his obscure intentions: "It was like hanging over a garden in the dark; nothing was to be made of the confusion of growing things, but one felt they were folded flowers, and their vague sweetness made the whole air their medium" (II, 295). This obscurity is a fine counterpart to the obscure moral intention which the Prince originally felt behind the American Poe-curtain of white mist.

In the end, the second Eden must always emerge from obscurity, but the obscurity will be friendly. The terrible loss of the first Eden does not necessarily, as some readers of *The Golden Bowl* have felt, make the second Eden false, empty, or impossible to face. In thinking of Maggie's future we must choose between a theory of fortunate fall and one of total cynicism. In this case, hope is deeper than despair.

The purgatory of metamorphosis, then, leads Maggie out of one garden and into another, and her sacred Sunday noon "sacrifice" for the sake of Charlotte's soul (a sacrifice made more poignant by the babbling Father Mitchell in the background and by the remembrance of Charlotte's Judas kiss on the terrace) carries all the religious intensity that witnesses to expulsions from and openings into Eden might anticipate. But the vehicle in which she rides through her gardens is still the carriage of the fairy tale, and it too rides through metamorphic and metaphoric magic. Maggie's most persistently painful pictures of her family relationships come in visions of vehicles and voyages. She sees Charlotte's entrance into the family in an image burdened with the humiliation of ignorance, reminiscent in its fright of Dostoievsky's famous dreams and, in content and structure, Frédéric's vision after the ball at Roseanette's in *L'Education sentimentale:*

> She might have been watching the family coach pass and noting that, somehow, Amerigo and Charlotte were pulling it while she and her father were not so much as pushing. They were seated inside together, dandling the Principino and holding him up to the windows, to see and be seen, like an infant positively royal; so that the exertion was *all* with the others. (II, 23-24)

So disturbing is this picture of royal sloth (paralleling that of Adam Verver's sprawling garden gods) that she sees herself "suddenly jump from the coach; whereupon, frankly, with the wonder of the sight, her eyes opened wider and her heart stood still for a moment" (II, 24). Her action is sure, but the form of the picture is still in doubt, and she must mold that with subsequent carriage trips in which real life complements image just as the climactic boat scene in *The Ambassadors* complements the many images of watery involvement in Strether's mind. A mere carriage ride from Eaton Square to Portland Place had grave import at the beginning of Part Two; and when Maggie begins to have the form of the picture as well as its substance clearly in mind, when she stays painfully in control of the consistency of her "plan," she remembers a former ride when she was prey to the Prince's easy magic:

> . . . and there were hours when it came to her that these days were a prolonged repetition of that night-drive, of weeks before, from the other house to their own, when he had tried to charm her, by his sovereign personal power, into some collapse that would commit her to a repudiation of consistency. (II, 139)

She must always resist coercion by charm, that of the Frog-Prince or that of the Father-King (which eventually imitates the silent control of Maggie herself by means of an imaginary silken halter around the neck of Charlotte). We know from our fairy tales how dangerous is the misuse of enchantment.

The image of royal sloth returns to haunt Maggie when her consciousness grows, and again the state of yielding one's self to metamorphosis, to the "lurches of the mystic train" (II, 95) carries with it the taste of humiliation:

> "We're in the train . . .; we've suddenly waked up in it and found ourselves rushing along, very much as if we had been put in during sleep—shoved like a pair of labelled boxes, into the van. . . . I'm moving without trouble—they're doing it all for us! (II, 69)

Maggie must eventually open the doors which will allow the right people in and let the right people out. She must refuse the magic lures of surrender in her father and of demonstrative love in the Prince. That the pain of knowledge accompanies the expulsion from the first Eden on this journey is emphasized by the proliferation of childhood imagery which serves naturally as a bridge between fairyland and Paradise. Adam Verver is persistently pictured as childlike in his absorptions, and it is this image, especially established in Part One, which Maggie must break through. The metaphorical translation of a projected trip with her father into the language of child growth shows Maggie that the journey is a false one:

> There had been, from far back . . . a plan that the parent and the child should "do something lovely" together, and they had recurred to it on occasion, nursed it and brought it up theoretically, though without as yet quite allowing it to put its feet to the ground. The most it had done was to try a few steps on the drawingroom carpet, with much attendance, on either side, much holding up and guarding, much anticipation, in fine, of awkwardness or accident. Their companions, by the same token, had constantly assisted at the performance, following the experiment with sympathy and gaiety, and never so full of applause, Maggie now made out for herself, as when the infant project had kicked its little legs most wildly—kicked them, for all the world, across the channel and half the Continent, kicked them over the Pyrenees and innocently crowed out some rich Spanish name. (II, 46)

It is when Maggie sees the journey itself as childish, not only in her own eyes, but in the tolerantly amused eyes of the Prince and Charlotte, who are always willing to reduce Maggie and her father to the state of childhood, that she sees most clearly the need for stern consistency in her plan.

How far from the first Eden Maggie has travelled in Part Two can best be seen by contrast with Part One. Backing down from the heights of Part Two, where Maggie maintains the dual role of observer and actor, we slide into the plodding mind of Fanny Assingham who must abandon composition when Maggie's deeper consciousness makes the imagery too rich for her blood.[2] Maggie's dual role, once she has confronted "the bad-faced stranger" (II, 237) of Evil, is most brilliantly assumed in the great terrace scene of Part Two where, looking in on a card game from outside, she sees before her "figures rehearsing some play of which she herself was the author" (II, 235). (By this allowance, James compensates his artists, and perhaps even himself, for their necessary loss of engagement in life.) She tracks and hunts her victims with her silent spear, with her silent pen, for, having the added role of involvement, she does not have open to her, as does Fanny, "the straight vindictive view, the rights of resentment, the rages of jealousy, the protests of passion" (II, 236). While Fanny bemoans the fact that her characters are "making a mess of such charming material" (I, 388-389), Maggie worries about saving lives. Maggie must not touch her loves, or, like Rappaccini's daughter, she might kill with her embrace; the poison must be secretly drained from the flowers before Eden can be revived.

Maggie's emergence into the light of consciousness is witnessed by the outgoing composer, Fanny Assingham, at Maggie's party. While Fanny stands "like one of the assistants in the ring at the circus," Maggie herself modestly skips "into the light" with "a show of pink stocking and . . . an abbreviation of white petticoat," ready at last to become the real Princess, "to fill out as a matter of course her appointed, her expected, her imposed character" (II, 71). She now feels the pea through the mattress, but, unlike the real Princess of the fairy tale, she cannot complain about it. Fanny, on the other hand, can complain about what she doesn't feel, and it is this complaint, as much inferior to the tone of Maggie's visions as is Colonel Assingham himself to Adam Verver as audience, which sets the tone of the first part of *The Golden Bowl*. Maggie herself senses Fanny's limitations once she herself can "boast of touching bottom" (II, 219).

Fanny cannot touch bottom because her mind looks for magic, resists metamorphosis, and flattens into a pattern.

Until we share the purgatory of metamorphosis with Maggie, until imagery becomes deep and varied and people are looked at, not romantically but realistically, we live in a world of Fanny's composition, of the picturesque, the static, a world which, despite Fanny's intelligence and because of her moral limitations, James condemns in all his great novels, in *The Portrait of a Lady*, *The Ambassadors*, *The Wings of the Dove*. The Prince is persistently, in the first part, seen by Maggie (her humoring of this vision does not soften its outline), by her father, by Fanny herself, as an item in Mrs. Verver's collection. Maggie is perfectly willing to share her father's vision: "His relation to the things he cares for—and I think it beautiful—is absolutely romantic" (I, 11). How completely this vision must be broken is Maggie's story, for here, as yet, she does not understand that the needs of a King, of a divinely permissive King, differ from those of a very human Princess.

The "taste" which substitutes in the Prince for morality, is adequate for Part One, where romance serves for reality and the picturesque for dynamism. But when Maggie enters her purgative experience, the Prince's taste, by his own admission, can no longer guide. This world demonstrates just how far Maggie's metamorphosis has taken her. While in Part Two she is busily opening doors of locked chambers, trains, launching ships freely into James's beloved waters of relationship, how poorly her conception of marriage as voyage began: " 'I've divided my faith into water-tight compartments. We must manage not to sink. . . . Why, it's the best cabin and the main deck and the engine-room and the steward's pantry! It's the ship itself—it's the whole line' " (I, 14-15). It is Maggie's romantic vision, of course, nourished ironically by her "familiarity with 'lines,' a command of 'own' cars, from an experience of continents and seas" (I, 15) which seals off her faith from the test of the real.

Meanwhile, Fanny Assingham encourages the pernicious romanticism of static vision. The Prince identifies Fanny's penchant toward pattern with that of the Ververs: "She had *made* his marriage, quite as truly as his papal ancestor had made his family—though he could scarce see what she had made it for unless because she too was perversely romantic" (I, 21). In his early section, the Prince, with Charlotte, sees clearly through the romance in the Verver vision, but it is for him to use it, not to change it. As long as Maggie and her father see the Prince as art and architecture, they remain, like the childlike Colonel Assingham, together in a "non-amphibious" state.

It is no accident that the first vision of Maggie's section is that of the outlandish pagoda of her "situation" in the center of her garden, and her first desire that of breaking through, of finding doors and windows. For Maggie does not abandon the romantic; she learns to use it, just as she does not abandon Eden or the fairy garden, but learns to open them to her greater needs. It is she who must replace Fanny as her own fairy godmother, and she makes passions of patterns, relationships of rituals. Fanny's constant clucking over poor Maggie's innocent ignorance is turned to full irony when Maggie, working in a higher ethic and aesthetic, leaves her behind. Maggie must do her own acting, because, as in *The Wings of the Dove*, those who surround innocence want, for their own comfort, to keep it isolated. Just as Fanny's composition depends upon keeping Maggie ignorant, so Charlotte can act only if she freezes Maggie's relationships to ritual:

> But it was all right—so Charlotte also put it: there was nothing in the world they (Maggie and Mr. Verver) liked better than these snatched felicities, little parties, long talks, with "I'll come to you to-morrow," and "No, I'll come to *you*," make-believe renewals of their own life. They were fairly, at times, the dear things, like children playing visits, playing at "Mr. Thompson" and "Mrs. Fane," each hoping that the other would really stay to tea. (I, 252)

We have seen before that it is just this recurrent image of childhood which Maggie must learn to resist in her growth to greatness. Even Fanny sees that the Prince and Charlotte were wrong to accept the innocence of Maggie as closed, to accept their idea of the guilelessness of the Ververs as something that could save them. It is not the isolated innocence of the Ververs, nor the isolating knowledge of the Prince and Charlotte which saves, but the expansion of innocence and knowledge, open to life, into love and wisdom.

Maggie's passage from victim to saviour (the familiar Jamesian pattern) is her emergence into greatness. She has an opportunity to go beyond Milly, to break the vision of herself as ritual. She breaks through the sentimentality of Fanny's picture of her "brave little piety" (I, 387) to its truth in relationship. All of the irony which metamorphosis carries turns upon the reversal of the cared for and cared by, the victims and the saviours. It is contained in the vague perception of Fanny concerning Maggie: "It will be *she* who'll see us through" (I, 280). This irony, which in the richest state of consciousness repeats experience to which unconsciousness has already been exposed, is strongly rooted in James's definition of greatness. At an early stage in the book, Maggie and Adam are having one of their talks which re-forms so effectively in Part Two. The subject of the talk is greatness, Charlotte's greatness, and Maggie who sees herself in comparison to Charlotte as "a small creeping thing" is, while defining Charlotte, defining herself as she finally will be, when she has, according to her prescription, acted upon her freedom and experienced the price of greatness: "I may be as good, but I'm not so great —and that's what we're talking about. She has a great imagination. She has, in every way, a great attitude. She has above all a great conscience" (I, 181-2). It is Maggie's "romance" which spreads its wings while Charlotte's "realism" is reduced to the painful shriek of a bobbing puppet at the end of a halter. Maggie, at the end of her great metamorphic process, is finally as real as she is right. It is she who restores Charlotte's dignity; it is she who has greatness of imagination, attitude, and conscience; it is she, at last who has become a real princess.

₰§ IX *The Lion in Us: The Contemporary Priority of Relationship*

"That Lion is all the baggage that I have." [1]

Saul Bellow

The tradition that we claim for James rested on a well known base: his persistent recognition of the difference between the cultural sophistication behind the European novel and character and the innocence that marked their American counterparts. Whenever he used this recognition, whether in criticism or in his novels, he implied that the continental philosophical rage for analysis and synthesis too often ignored the dramatic controls of a sensitive morality. Consequently, the French novel fell on the one hand into a crude romanticism in which demonic obsessions, systematized analyses and categories of thought and passion, or the idyllic escape from moral complexities into varieties of pastoralism tended to depersonalize the novel by allowing temperament to absorb character and the absolutism of melodrama or of the ideal to overwhelm conscience. On the other hand it courted, with naturalism, a scientific reduction of consciousness, of the individual case.

The English novel, in which James saw a strong ethical control, was beset by a rage for correction based on the assumption of certain moral systems. The trajectory of the Austen heroine begins in ignorance and ends in correction. Knightley stands surely and patiently at the close of the journey. In his major phase, James was not interested in this kind of comedy. By changing "ignorance" to "innocence" (terms which he frequently used and carefully distinguished for the sake of an "American" or "European" application), he opened consciousness to the strain of choosing between moral possibilities and of choosing through a whole lifetime. This is a morality that creates a very different pattern from that emerging from the province-to-Paris initiation at the heart of the realistic novel of the nineteenth century, whatever superficial similarities may seem to suggest.

We remember that James balanced his famous complaints about the American novel with excitement about its possibilities. Though it lacked the historical sophistications of an aesthetic or ethical base (a base which could only be imported), it offered as many advantages as disadvantages to the new novelist. From one point of view it may seem regressive to have to concern oneself with "innocence abroad" rather than correction, thematic analysis, or synthesis, yet it was just this elementalism that allowed the flexible psychological base of human relationships to become the central pivot for the American novel. The discovery of this pivot was the source of James's tremendous optimism for the future of the novel. His essential temper was not sociological, and hence it was not depressed by the problems of historical decay. Stephen Spender's hypothesis [2] that James retreated, however nobly, from threats of the present is probably not as valid, at least from the literary standpoint, as the fact that he reacted against the past. It is important for the emphasis we are supporting here, to contend that the particular and necessary historical perspective behind the consciousness of decay actually removes the James novel from novels such as *Buddenbrooks, Howard's End, Parade's End,*[3] in which the strength of relational morality weakens with the decline of social morality. It moves closer to future-oriented novels like *Henderson the Rain King* and *The Deer Park,* for all their Laurentian frenzy of search for new nervous dimensions. Philip Rahv sums up the uniquely "pure" quality of James's mind in an interesting essay:

> There never was a writer so immersed in personal relations, and his consistency in this respect implies an anti-historical attitude. This helps to explain the peculiarities of his consciousness, which is intellectual yet at the same time indifferent to general ideas, deeply comprehensive yet unattached to any open philosophical motive.[4]

And there is yet another aspect of James's resistance to violation of the novel by history and philosophy. If we temporarily adopt the categories of Northrop Frye[5] for the sake of further distinguishing James's view of the "old" novel we might say that the "old" French novel leans much more heavily to the side of anatomy (Flaubert actually termed *Madame Bovary* an "anatomy" [6]) than does the "old" English novel. In France, Stendhal and Proust mark approximately the bounds of "the great tradition" while Austen and James might serve as analogous bounds for the English novel. Whenever an independently maintained idea, such as the search for the absolute, or the search for time lost, is nourished by the social scene, we can expect a strong "anti-social" strain as a counter-reaction. The Idea is formed, after all, in the isolated laboratory or in the cork-lined room, and it is by nature obsessive. Its flourishing depends upon the ultimate *destruction* of the social and domestic relations surrounding it, with the accompanying death and decay: its immortality needs to be set off by reminders of mortality. In the writing of a novel, the directive Idea is the self-conscious process of composition hovering over what is being written.

This antagonism between idea and social milieu which amounts to the exaggeration of romance and the analysis of anatomy warring against the novel, is certainly not evident on the English side.[7] Whatever Idea we find here tends to melt into the social situation; we have assimilation rather than antagonism, and this makes a very different novel. It is perhaps this distinction that James sensed when he wrote:

> When we others of the Anglo-Saxon race are vulgar we are, handsomely and with the best conscience in the world, vulgar all through, too vulgar to be in any degree literary, and too much so therefore to be critically reckoned with at all. The French are different—they separate their sympathies, multiply their possibilities, observe their shades, remain more or less outside of their worst disasters. They mostly contrive to get the *idea,* in however dead a faint, down into the lifeboat. They may lose sight of the stars, but they save in some such fashion as that their intellectual souls.[8]

James was partisan to the English side, and his discomfort at the occasional splits he felt Eliot made between drama and philosophy was a manifestation of his partisanship. His own characters are plagued over and over again by the temptation to idea (which demands the separation of the romantic from the real) on the one hand and to naturalism on the other. But because they are transmuted into round characters, differences in cultural textures become as complex as the human mind itself. The American romance of innocence is both a trap and a salvation; the continental sophistication of naturalism is treacherous and educative. James's own realism had to establish its pressures and validity without the aid, in the later novels, of cups and saucers. The fact that we drink from the golden bowl meant that metaphor had to become the stuff, the material density, that accompanied the dailyness of Puritan self-examination, the moral "business" of life. The materializing of metaphorical reality through the intense working of consciousness in character is a common feature of the modern novelistic texture, and it leads us to ask about the relevance of James's realism for the future of fiction. What can James, who himself has become an annoying Proust to the Robbe-Grillets, mean for the "new" novel?

In a recent article George Steiner describes the modern "retreat from the word" as symptomatic of the scientism of modern literature as well as life.[9] Joyce, Faulkner, and Durrell, in his view, become our major rescuers from decay of the literate in literature. Here, at least implicitly, is another contribution to the growing list of assertions about the death of the novel. The retreat from the word affects the novel as gravely as the societal retreat described by Trilling or the ideological retreat, the "coyness toward the things of the mind"[10] that has marked American literature especially. But the retreat from the word is in itself dwarfed by the larger retreat from relationship. I think it is important to see this withdrawal as one that could have grave consequences for the modern novel, because its recognition might lead us to positive paths other than those of the political-ideological or of the French "reist" school which prefers the dialectic of idea and pattern to that of personality.

Joyce, from this aspect, becomes for the contemporary novel more of a villain than a hero, and even his greatest admirers, following the lead of the "moral" critics,[11] have confessed that Joyce has as much killed as created the modern novel. Joyce works with the relaxation of consciousness; the James relational novel depends upon a consciousness that conquers the temptations of sleep, death, and free association. Joyce's characters, for all their yearning for the great standard relationships, are isolated by the mythopoeic abstraction of personal psychology and drama. As the dependence on word becomes more and more extreme, the retreat from relationship becomes more and more inevitable. As the word makes the world more private, it makes character more public. Joyce's tech-

nique makes ritual out of the mind as Lawrence's eventually made
ritual out of relationship.

On the other hand, the retreat of the French experimentalists,
taking its starting point from the rejection of the Balzacian dossier
and the Proustian sensibility, turns psychology and moral drama not
to myth but to empirical perception. Despite James's open invitations
to experimentation, I can imagine nothing so horrible to his novelistic taste than the novels of Robbe-Grillet. He would have seen in
the new novel of France a heavy strain of naturalism that pretended
to center upon man, but obliterated character. (Isn't character,
after all, the measure and quality of *control* we have over our com-
pulsions, of resistance to them, of our renunciations?) To make a
documented map of the mind is to level the land of the novel. To
claims of concentration on the individual case, James would answer
that any case, without personality and the moral sense,[12] has lost its
representative value. Ultimately, James would probably have directed
the same accusations against the school of Robbe-Grillet as against
the naturalist ideal: it deliberately cuts off the source of felt life,
and the amorality of disengagement between author and subject that
destroys tone is more appropriate for science than for literature.
This is not to say, of course, that the objective school is not possible
or, at times even, possibly exciting. (Its aims are most eloquently
and readably expressed by Nathalie Sarraute.) [13] But for all its honesty, we must question whether or not it will work for the extension
of the novel's potenitality. Though the plaint irritates the "reistic"
practitioners, it is this "objective" tendency (or subjectivism deper-
sonalized) that makes us ask: "How long can the novel survive when
character is material rather than moral?"

There is perhaps a stronger contrast to be made, one which concerns distinction rather than evaluation. The major work of novelists like Faulkner and Joyce belongs, roughly, to the literature that
plays man's actions and thoughts against the ultimate questions of
Life and Death—literature of generic survival, whether of body or
mind. Like the organizing idea of the French novel, this literature
tends to be anti-social (Dilsey's apocalyptic summation: "I've seed
de first en de last" allows her to endure relationship, not discover
it). This is a strain which works basically through the positions of
isolation rather than through those of alliance; here character reaction is closer to ritual than relationship. It is a tenor that is strong in

the American novel where so much of social representation is allegorical rather than dramatically flexible.

Morality in Hawthorne and Melville is basically metaphysical, uncompromising, and elemental. It is a morality of survival rather than that of daily living, and it of course reflects the American obsession with survival. Like the morality of Othello, it can not deal with the psychological adjustments of the middle roads, but breaks completely or survives whole, inviolate, and unrelated. Unpardonable sins are not committed or forgiven by the individual case, but are hatched and immortalized by the serpents in all our breasts.

The pastoral strain in the classic American novel, so frequently explored of late, is again a symptom of ultimate concern about the beginnings and ends of morality (or an escape from moral concern altogether) in contrast to the active morality of daily relationship. The child, the isolated spectator, and the man made myth are typical registers of the literature of survival which contains a large element of fable. (*The Marble Faun* is, from this view, much closer to a novel like William Golding's *Lord of the Flies* than it is really to *The Wings of the Dove*.) Unlike the Strethers of growing consciousness the emphatic characters in the literature of survival are most often obviously representative as very small and close to nature (like Lena Grove or Billy Budd) or exaggeratedly large to the point of godlike mythical extension (like Ahab or H. C. Earwicker). Their meaning to themselves and to each other is filtered through a general historical or poetic perspective. Although Joyce is more concerned with ultimates of mind than of morality, he retreats so surely from relationship that his work may be said to share the perspective of survival. And the concern with sensational survival, when pushed to absurd extremes, can by itself mark the difference between Kerouac's static hipster picaresque and the relational picaresque of Mailer and Bellow.

In a recent essay on Hawthorne, Lionel Trilling suggests that James's sensibility is in many ways obsolete in an age dominated by Kafka's "subversive" strain. Obviously James's novels have nothing at all to do with the literature of the underground man, and no one cared less than James that "God was dead." The metaphysical assumptions of existentialist literature would alienate James. But it is a mistake, I think, to imply that it is the thin rendering of an objective world which would bother him. If the line of Kafka emphasizes the "autonomy of spirit," that of James might be said to lead us to the "autonomy of relationship." The isolationism of the underground man is not found in the James heroine, but her relationships, in their supersocial determination, so strongly shape moral values that one might call them metaphysically structured.[14]

When possible escape routes away from the death of the novel are sketched, there is a prior path that should not be easily marked as too conventional for our shell-shocked sensibilities. The "new" American novel which James defined by theory and practice is not old-fashioned; it must be, as long as the novel survives, one of the richest routes of all. Even the modern renaissance of the picaresque spirit (Saul Bellow, Norman Mailer, Herbert Gold, J. D. Salinger, etc.) is significantly indicative of the desire to be free of the "certain moral scheme" [15] for the sake of constructing a new morality based upon recognition of the priority of relationship. It is often assumed that the times have thrust the anti-hero and his floating world upon us. But in the most thoughtful (and at the same time playful) of the novels which explore the security of stereotyped social or moral positions, in *The Victim,* for example, modesty of status is as much a personal choice as a cultural consequence. The rejection of the old heroism is an assertion of the new, a plea for honesty, flexibility, and human involvement, and it affects the novel's form as much as the hero's life. Henderson sheds his pseudo-giantism as he consummates relationship, but his size had always indicated his capacity for a positive human commitment. The Gargantuan parody, because it leads to the most personal concerns, only points up how much closer, from another view, Henderson is to Strether than we may imagine. Henderson's Europe is Africa, and his Mme de Vionnet is Dahfu. (Enlargement of character and scene tells us something about the quantitative and qualitative changes that a lapse of time forces upon the drama of relationship for the sake of making it felt.) The modern relational hero, like Henderson, Mailer's Sergius O'Shaughnessy, or Malamud's Levin, comes into the adult world a self-created orphan, free to think of "Sex as Time; and Time as the connection of new circuits." [16] The spatial view is static and irrelevant and America can become Africa in one easy step of Henderson's boot. (It is interesting that Joyce, so removed from the relational novelist, has been consistently terms a "spatial" novelist by Joseph Frank, Harry Levin, and T. S. Eliot, among others.) [17] But the temporal view is dramatic and allows meaning, ends, and beginnings to relationship.[18] Bellow and Mailer, Lawrence and James, not strange but vital allies, are all searching in the state of relatedness for the connection of new moral circuits.

It is a search, it seems to me, which will guarantee the permanence of James. Novelists and critics who are willing to theorize about the "death" of the classical novel and what it means for modern fiction, Nathalie Sarraute, Mary McCarthy, Saul Bellow, Steven Marcus, have all described the atmosphere between the modern novelist and traditional novelistic materials, and between the novel and its readers, as highly suspicious. That is, according to Nathalie Sarraute, the reader of novels will no longer accept the Balzacian world of crowded data. Mary McCarthy can only project the fantasy that someone might someday write again:

> At five o'clock in the afternoon, in the capital of the Province of Y., a tall man with an umbrella was knocking at the door of the governor's residence.[19]

Whereas the French theorists seem to concentrate more upon aesthetic literary changes, the American critics focus often upon the social causes behind these changes. (These are obviously the two countries most engaged in practicing and justifying experimentation in prose fiction.) Mary McCarthy, for example, claims that reality itself has been so fantastic that the novelist can no longer rival it. The disappearance of memorable "character" is caused by the absence of social dimension in the novel.[20] In an interesting essay, which can be read with Lionel Trilling's classic "Reality in America," [21] Saul Bellow talks about a novelistic "dissociation of sensibility":

> In Balzac and Flaubert and the great Russian masters the realistic externals were intended to lead inward. I suppose one might say that now the two elements, the inward and the external, have come apart.
> In what we call the novel of sensibility the intent of the writer is to pull us into an all-sufficient consciousness which he, the writer, governs absolutely. In the realistic novel today the writer is satisfied with an art of externals.
> . . . .
> What is happening now is that the intrinsic excitement of the facts themselves has become intense, and the literary imagination must rival the power of the real.[22]

Actually, I think there is less pressure for facts in fiction, for what Bellow calls "hard knowledge," than there has ever been. It was

Balzac who had this burden, and Bellow's argument almost contradicts that of Nathalie Sarraute. If the modern novelist constructs a shell it is probably to protect soft knowledge from sentimentality. As Mary McCarthy has pointed out, the fact in fiction is anachronistic. Obviously we can get our information in a hundred better places outside of the novel. Certainly we have to agree with Steven Marcus who notes, in a fine article, that the constant development of the modern novel (Golding, Malamud, Bellow, Updike) has been toward a more poetic texture.[23] It seems ironic that in this climate, James has been so often rejected by writers as a guide for the perplexed future (at the same time that he has been so ardently fêted by critics). Bellow writes:

> The living heirs of Henry James and Virginia Woolf do not do very well, and I'm afraid that they largely deserve their neglect. They have receded altogether too far from externals, from observation, in their desire for mental independence and free sensibility. They give us very little information.

It is true that James himself retreated more and more from surface realism, but as he did so, his moral lessons (soft knowledge) became less and less hermetic; they became more documentary as they became more dramatic, for they had to give a compensatory illusion for the thinning of social detail. He ought not, with a proper emphasis (and with proper disciples), be grouped with Virginia Woolf and her heirs as a "selfish saint" of literature. The so-called novel of sensibility, as James writes it, in which the social and spiritual spheres are spanned by relationship, should have a great deal of relevance for our time. If the cold war and the memory of Auschwitz make reality too unreal for fiction, we can use, and *do* use in the modern novel a theme and a structure which is, as James discovered, ideally suited for a society with insecure or artificial moral and social traditions. They anchor us to a reality that has a personal reference and a universal validity, one that seems immune (without being cowardly or escapist) to shifting balances of power.

Just as the unreality of the fairy setting in *The Golden Bowl* centers consciousness on the vitally real morality of relationship, so too the rootlessness of Henderson's Gargantuan capacities turns him away from the unreality of his life and allows him to go freely forth in search of the reality of relationship. With Mailer, Bellow sponsors, as part of this turning, a revaluation of Time, the irrelevancy of Space, and the capacity of the orphan. Time need not lead us on "a sick and hasty ride, helpless, through a dream into oblivion," but "can be arrested by a thing or two," [24] by art, by relationship, by relationship in art. The stopping and molding of Time in the land of Dahfu makes Time in the Old World seem strange to the return ing Henderson. He has relinquished, with all good picaresque heroes, the world of habit, but like Christ and unlike the traditional pica-resque hero, he spreads out in Space only for depth, not width; he seeks variety not for entertainment but for meaning. He must lose his old life in order to gain life itself, leave "parents . . . wives . . . girls . . . children . . . farm . . . animals . . . habits . . . money . . . music lessons . . . drunkenness . . . prejudices . . . brutality . . . teeth . . . face" (p. 5), trade the world of the pig for the world of the lion. He takes a one-way ticket to the continent and gets his teeth so squarely into life that he breaks, literally, the bridge work that connected him to the old world. He is not an "heir," but a "bum," as much an orphan as the black baby his daughter Ricey finds (p. 8). Like the James heroine he is freed by money and must make meaning out of the terror freedom brings.

In turning from America, Henderson broods: "There is a curse on this land. There is something bad going on. Something is wrong. There is a curse on this land" (p. 35). The curse of the fertility cult, so familiar to our Eliotic conscience, is transplanted from the Old World into the New. Henderson drags the shallow nouveau riche American temperament to Europe, and then in Africa, he thinks:

> I had sensed from the first that I might find things . . . which were of old, which I saw when I was still innocent and have longed for ever since, for all my life, and without which *I could not make it.* My spirit was not sleeping then, I can tell you, but was saying, Oh, ho, ho, ho, ho, ho, ho. (pp. 90-91)

Now on the threshold of this second Eden, he is equipped by his picaresque heritage with enough money for freedom, enough capacity for consciousness, enough desire for "high conduct" (p. 234).

Because Henderson relates to the comic picaresque heroes of Swift, Fielding, and Rabelais, his capacity for consciousness is mani-fest largely in physical properties. Willatale tells Henderson: "you have a great capacity [sic], indicated by your largeness, and espe-cially your nose" (p. 74). The great and broken nose reacts to life,

on its own and is as joyously related to his phallic consciousness as
the nose of Tristram Shandy is to his. Dahfu makes constant reference to the analogy between anatomical and metamorphic capacity
in his encouragement of Henderson, and Henderson himself is
drawn to the great capacity of his wife Lily who gave him twin boys
and eats as heartily as he does (p. 82).

Though the world of comic physical giantism is not the world of
James, Henderson's physical capacity is ultimately translated into the
moral capacity for relationship. Two descriptions, which begin as
physical, illustrate this: the first of Henderson by Mtalba, the woman
who loves him, is quoted by Romilayu, "The woman of Bittahness
who loves the great wrestler, the man who is like two men who have
grown together, come to him in the night" (p. 92); the second of
Dahfu by Henderson, who loves him, "Like all people who have a
strong gift of life, he gave off almost an extra shadow" (p. 185).
These images are merely promises of capacity; they become real at
the end of Henderson's odyssey when he becomes permanently "like
two men who have grown together" and carries with him the shadow
of Dahfu.

The task he faces, like any hero or heroine of the relational novel,
is the breaking up of ritual, rigidity, and fixity in life and the opening up of the soul to relationship. When, in the crucial encounters
with Atti, the lion, Henderson is ready to admit a failure to "lion-
ize" himself, Dahfu scolds him in these terms:

> Oh . . . Mr. Henderson, Mr. Henderson! Is this the man who
> spoke of rising from a grave of solitude? Who recited me the
> poem of the little fly on the green leaf in the setting sun? Who
> wished to end Becoming? Is this the Henderson who flew half
> around the world because he had a voice which said *I want?*
> And now, because his friend Dahfu extends a remedy to him, falls
> down? You dismiss my relationship? (p. 235)

The refusal to open himself to the metamorphosis which relationship demands will mean the death of his spirit. Lay aside your
fixity, warns Dahfu. Relate freely to the lion, and then out to the
universe. The same temptations of the static world that we found in
James and Lawrence, portraits, theories, and ritual of death, we find
in the path of Henderson. Like Gulliver, despite comic proportion
he is related to the hero with a thousand faces who descends into
the underworld (the lion's den) or again is exiled to the land of the

Houyhnhms and comes back with what Henderson calls a "service motivation." However, he returns not with a curse for the smells of the real world, nor with a golden fleece, but only with a lion cub named Dahfu for baggage, only relationship as the secret of life. He also brings an orphan who will recreate the relational process. His motivation to become a doctor has changed from service to the kind of relationship which begins with understanding the connection of parts to wholes in man and between men, and between men and the universe.

Henderson's temptation to death and to ritual comes significantly after his failure at "service" in the land of the Arnewi:

> Thus we started off toward the Wariri while I was thinking about the burial of Oedipus at Colonus—but he at least brought people luck after he was dead. At that time I might almost have been willing to settle for this. (p. 101)

He realizes early the dangers of the ideological temptation in Lily and says pertinently of himself: "That's how it is with my ideas; they seem to get strong while I weaken" (p. 85). The temptation of the picturesque and the portrait is faced easily and efficiently by Henderson. He separates from his friend Charlie in Africa because: "Photography is not one of my interests" (p. 38). The portrait is played with as symbolically in this novel as in a James piece. Lily must have life in a portrait, but Henderson's sense of reality is too vital for that security and he uses a family portrait to tempt Dahfu into a bet.

But it is to the positive temptation offered by the lion, the great and good temptation to relational metamorphosis, that Henderson must yield. Henderson is terrified that failure with the lion will make him "lose . . . [his] connection" with Dahfu, and that would be the most painful loss possible (p. 229). Dahfu himself says to Henderson:

> Sungo . . . I also am close to you. It is very mutual. But I require more deep relationship. I desire to be understood and communicated to. We have to develop an underlying similarity which lies within you by connection with the lion. (p. 230)

When Dahfu expands upon his theories about the relationship of outer appearance to inner character and of the parts of anatomy to each other and to the universe, he begins to sound like the first affirmative black disciple of D. H. Lawrence. It is a dynamic sense of relatedness with which Dahfu seeks to infuse Henderson, a dynamism that comes from the vital centers, from the "freedom of the intercostal muscles and . . . abdominal flexibility" (p. 230). More important, it will, in the great relational tradition, "make consciousness to shine" (p. 230). This consciousness, however, is not the white but the black consciousness, for Dahfu again follows Lawrence, in asserting that in the good relationship, wholesome love, ego-emphasis is buried in the rhythm of life (p. 232). This awareness contrasts with the kind of false knowledge that passes for consciousness in the sophisticated world of Charlotte Stant and the Prince but really isolates instead of connecting:

> I intend to loosen you up, Sungo, because you are so contracted. This is why we were running. The tendency of your conscious is to isolate self. This makes you extremely contracted and self-recoiled . . . (p. 234)

When Henderson returns to his old world, he carries with him the ritualistic lion of relatedness whose existence will remind him to connect the circuits.

He returns gladly to Lily who, with Dahfu, has been identified as a worthy relational partner all the way through the novel, and he writes to her that she should get rid of the pigs. Unlike Don Quixote, he humiliates the pigs before they can humiliate him, for he understands the difference between the I-Thou of the lion world and the I-It of the pig world. And like Strether, he carries back with him an image of his own Mme de Vionnet and a knowledge that consciousness can change life, can "make it to shine." He wonders how he had ever been interested in hunting the animal world he now relates to:

> Myself, I used to have a certain interest in hunting, but as I grew older it seemed a strange way to relate to nature. What I mean is, a man goes into the external world, and all he can do with it is to shoot it? (p. 84)

Surely one of Bellow's most persistent novelistic messages is the sanctity of relating. With the recognition that life is absurd (that *homo ludens* is at best *animal ridens*),[25] Augie March, as a new Columbus, launches his boat into the waters of relationship and discovery, refuses to drown consciousness in the sea of absurdity surrounding us. This he can shore against his ruin. Henderson's own yearnings have been transformed; he remembers one of the ideas on the lost pages of his letter to Lily:

> In one I think I said, or maybe I merely thought it, "I had a voice that said, I want! I want! I? It should have told me *she* wants, he wants, *they* want. And moreover, it's love that makes reality. The opposite makes the opposite. (p. 253)

As in James, love makes reality as it makes morality. Henderson is at last satisfied to admit: "That lion is all the baggage that I have . . ." (p. 300).

Bellow's latest novel, *Herzog,* so different in texture and intellectual weight from any novel of James as to preclude some kinds of comparison, nevertheless relies dramatically and philosophically on a new Strether's late awakening to the truth, possibility, and necessity of genuine and flexible personal involvements. Like Strether, Moses Herzog stops at the border of the Promised Land and his positive awareness is born from a negative past. Historical age and personal temperament, the nature and profession of Bellow's hero, his closeness to our culture, have radically changed the costume, but the same flesh is underneath. A wilder joy replaces the calm of knowing renunciation, but the same enemies have been defeated: Ideology— metaphysical, ethical and aesthetic, public and private, the constant rationalizations and justifications by which we formally shape experience before it is lived, and which prevents its life; and Apocalypse —the violent expectation of meaning and hope outside of the individual case. Bellow, as forcefully as Camus, has asserted that to be a man, neither more nor less, is far more difficult than to be more or less. Asa Leventhal discovers that it is easier to be a victim than a man. James was not haunted by the Nietzschian view of civilized catastrophe, but for him, as well as for novelists like Bellow, the old moralities, the old certain schemes, the old religious security that was also, by its ghetto smugness, a social security, the escape to ideologies and apocalypses, are measures which belittle and dishonor the relationships that both life and the life of the novel depend upon. The death of Herzog's letters initiates Herzog into a new life and the reader into the meaning of the novel. The final moment of silence justifies the sound and the fury of all the words.

ᴥᕔ X *Conclusion*

A single immense cannon, at a tremendous distance said
something. Something sulky. Aroused in its sleep and protest-
ing. But it was not a signal to begin anything. Too heavy.
Firing at something at a tremendous distance. At Paris,
maybe, or the North Pole, or the moon! They were capable
of that, those fellows!

It would be a tremendous piece of frightfulness to hit the
moon. Great gain in prestige. And useless. There was no
knowing what they would not be up to, as long as it was
stupid and useless. And, naturally, boring. One went on fight-
ing to get rid of those bores—as you would get rid of a bore
in a club.[1]

Ford Madox Ford

Since James's death the house of fiction has been filled with a
great variety of watchers. The fragmenting successors of Joyce and
the Robbe-Grillet school have preferred to pull down the blinds.
When the world is seen it is often mocked by farce which allows a
comfortable distance between author and subject. The modern farcical vision forces a retreat from the drama of relationship to the static
impressionism of the private mind. But it is not even the mind that
rules; it is the eye. Or it is the ear. Since Ortega Y Gasset articulated
these tendencies,[2] everyone recognizes that we are facing the frighten-
ing (if at times fascinating) effects of the dehumanization of the
novel. The *"homme moyen sensuel"* has become no man at all. Dramatic consciousness of character has been obliterated by an attempt
to objectify the passive mind. The proliferation of the comically
obsessed or psychopathic hero, the isolated voyeur, who controls our
vision in modern fiction is perhaps the result of the crumbling of the
social pillar of the classical novel, traditionally shaped by the tension
between society and the individual. The antagonism has necessarily
shifted to abnormal individual vs. a death-like norm, character has

shifted from unique complexity to archetypal extremism, and dominant tone from irony to farce. With no moral anchor, the Lucky Jims
and the Billy Liars use people with few guilty hangovers. Their
fantasies hurt. The morality of relationship, the heart of the James
novel, seems to some to belong to another era.

In one of his most poignant reminiscences, James recalls that as a
boy, just after, himself, crossing from America to Europe, he witnessed a farcical theatrical entertainment at the very moment the
ship "Atlantic" was overdue. The audience carried the burden of
human concern into the theatre. Mr. Mouser, the hero of the farce,
who cavorted about the stage chased by a troupe of laundresses,
feared only a humiliating capture. Just after the curtain fell, Mr.
Mouser, still in his garments of farce, appeared suddenly at the foot-
lights and announced breathlessly: "Ladies and gentlemen, I rejoice
to be able to tell you that the good ship Atlantic is safe!" James
describes the reaction:

> The house broke into such plaudits, so huge and prolonged a roar
> of relief, as I had never heard the like of and which gave me my
> first measure of a great immediate public emotion—even as the
> incident itself to-day reminds me of the family-party smallness of
> the old New York, those happy limits that could make us all
> care, and care to fond vociferation, for the same thing at once.[3]

The individual case has paled in the darkness of a gruesome historical scene, which has "democratized" social and moral reaction
and expectation. The reading public, as many critics have noted, no
longer feels those "happy limits." Yet it would seem that with the
crumbling of the theatrical walls, and so many of the old moralities,
more than ever the novel which features the dignity of the individual case responding in free and dramatic attempts at human connection gives us something "classical" that "could make us all care
. . . for the same thing at once." Surely the novel can still bring us
together despite mocking farce. Take account of all the wonderful
irony at the end of Malamud's *A New Life,* still, when those who
fear the responsibility of relational sensibility mockingly ask: "Why
take that load on yourself?", Levin can give an answer that is, like
Isabel's, ennobling in its refusal to allow desperation and absurdity to
overwhelm the sense of personal "density": "Because I can, you son
of a bitch." [4]

Granted his prejudices, James assures us of at least one fit lifeboat. The question that he inevitably leads us to ask is a vital one: "Ultimately, without a concern for the deeply human and conscious relationship at its center, can the novel 'help us to live'; will it become, otherwise for us, both useless and boring?"

❧ Notes

Frontispiece

1. *The Portrait of a Lady* (New York, 1908-17), I, 54. All future references will be to this edition.

Preface

2. See the chapter on James in *Boon, The Mind of the Race, The Wild Assess of the Devil,* and *The Last Trump* (London, 1915), pp. 84-128. The section is reprinted, with James' reaction, in the more available *Henry James and H. G. Wells: A Record of Their Friendship,* ed. Leon Edel and Gordon N. Ray (Urbana, 1958), pp. 234-260.

3. Frank O'Connor, *The Mirror in the Roadway* (New York, 1956), p. 224.

4. "Problems for the Modern Critic of Literature," *Hudson Review,* IX (Autumn, 1956), 350.

5. "Maule's Curse," *In Defense of Reason* (Denver, 1947), p. 306.

6. See Lionel Trilling, Introduction to *The Princess Casamassima* (New York, 1948), reprinted in *The Liberal Imagination* (New York, 1950); and Introduction to the Chiltern Library edition of *The Bostonians* (London, 1953), reprinted in *The Opposing Self* (New York, 1955). Irving Howe, Introduction to the Modern Library Edition of *The Bostonians* (New York, 1956), reprinted with alterations, in Irving Howe, *Politics and the Novel* (New York, 1957). The reader should also consult Howe's perceptive "correction" of Trilling's views on *The Princess Casamassima* which also appears in *Politics and the Novel,* pp. 139-156.

7. *The American Henry James* (New Brunswick, 1957), p. xi.

8. Austin Warren, in "Symbolic Imagery in the Later Novels of Henry James," *Rage for Order* (Ann Arbor, 1948), terms the late novels metaphysical, but treats them aesthetically.

9. See George Santayana, *Character and Opinion in the United States* (New York, 1956), pp. 24-25.

10. *The Image of Europe in Henry James* (Dallas, 1958), p. 105.

11. Preface to *The Portrait of a Lady* in *The Art of the Novel*, ed. R. P. Blackmur (New York, 1934), p. 46.

Chapter I

1. "The Story in It," in *Stories of Writers and Artists,* ed. F. O. Matthiessen (Norfolk, 1949), p. 341.

2. "The Figure in the Carpet," *ibid.,* p. 304.

3. *Ibid.,* p. 306.

4. *Ibid.,* p. 304.

5. *Ibid.,* p. 294.

6. It is a concern that, while always with him, became more and more basic to his artistic form as he approached the late novels. *The Portrait of a Lady* (1881) gives us our first strong sense of how James will manipulate his "relational" heroines. Though we cannot talk of the refinement of this center in terms of "progress," we may, I think, argue that James' greatest and most important method in his own eyes as well as in those of his reader) fully used this theme as structure.

7. "The Story in It," *loc. cit.*

8. *Ibid.,* p. 337.

9. *Ibid.,* p. 338.

10. *Ibid.,* p. 338-339.

11. *Ibid.,* p. 339.

12. *Ibid.,* p. 341.

13. It is interesting to read, in conjunction with this, the late story, "The Velvet Glove."

14. *Loc. cit.*

Chapter II

1. "Emile Zola," *Notes on Novelists* (New York, 1914), p. 36.

2. "Daniel Deronda: A Conversation," *Partial Portraits* (London, 1905), p. 92.

3. I think that F. R. Leavis' patient attitude towards James's tendency to speak in vague terms like "felt life" and "taste" is a sane and rewarding one:

> It doesn't take a great deal of reflection to establish that 'life' is a large word and doesn't admit of definition. But some of the most important words we have to use don't admit of definition. And this truth holds of literary criticism . . . (Preface to *Selected Literary Criticism of Henry James,* ed. Morris Shapira [London, 1963], p. xvii).

4. D. H. Lawrence, a surprisingly frequent critical ally of James, censures Flaubert for this same poverty of registers in his review of Verga's *Mastro-don Gesualdo,* in *Phoenix* (London, 1936), p. 226.

5. This expression applies to Kate Croy and is to be found in the

preface to *The Wings of the Dove* in *The Art of the Novel,* ed. R. P. Blackmur (New York, 1937), p. 297.

6. These celebrated definitions appear in the preface to *The American, ibid.,* pp. 31-32. Lionel Trilling, "Art and Fortune," *The Liberal Imagination,* p. 260, brings the terms into a proper Jamesian focus and balance when he expands upon these definitions to emphasize that the pleasant, the charming, the distant, and the ideal are not qualities to be identified with romance, but rather that romance stands for "the world of unfolding possibility, for that which, when brought to actuality, is powerfully operative. It is thus a synonym for the will in its creative aspect, especially in its aspect of *moral* creativeness, as it subjects itself to criticism and conceives for itself new states of being." But isolated from the real, this force remains powerless for the novel as for character.

7. Preface to *The Portrait of a Lady, ibid.,* p. 45.

8. *Partial Portraits,* pp. 406-407.

9. *The Selected Letters of John Keats,* ed. Lionel Trilling (New York, 1956), p. 103.

10. "The Last French Novel," *Notes and Reviews* (Cambridge, Mass., 1921) pp. 225-226.

11. Preface to *Portrait, The Art of the Novel,* pp. 46-47.

12. *The Notebooks of Henry James,* ed. F. O. Matthiessen and K. B. Murdock (New York, 1955), pp. 225-226.

13. Preface to *Portrait, The Art of the Novel,* pp. 46-47.

14. Brothers de Goncourt," *Essays in London and Elsewhere* (London, 1893), pp. 202-203.

15. This term will be explored in Section 4 of this chapter.

16. "Nana," *The Future of the Novel,* ed. Leon Edel (New York, 1956), p. 93.

17. *Ibid.,* p. 96.

18. *Loc. cit.*

19. "Zola," *Notes on Novelists,* p. 49.

20. *Ibid.,* p. 54.

21. *Ibid.,* p. 60.

22. *Ibid.,* p. 54.

23. "George Sand," *French Poets and Novelists* (London, 1908), p. 184.

24. *Ibid.,* p. 185. This judgment is shared by Flaubert in views which he expresses strongly and openly in his letters to George Sand.

25. *Ibid.,* p. 175.

26. "Ivan Turgenieff," *French Poets,* p. 217.

27. *Ibid.,* p. 219.

28. "Gustave Flaubert," *Notes on Novelists,* p. 96.

29. *Selected Letters,* ed. Francis Steegmuller (New York, 1953), p. 151.

30. *Ibid.,* p. 140.

31. O'Connor, *Mirror in the Roadway,* p. 184.

32. *Essays in London,* p. 158.
33. "Gustave Flaubert," *Notes on Novelists,* pp. 67 ff.
34. *Ibid.,* p. 97.
35. *Ibid.,* p. 76.
36. "Minor French Novelists: The Goncourts," *Literary Reviews and Essays,* ed. Albert Mordell (New York, 1957), p. 162.
37. Quoted in Leon Edel, *Henry James: The Middle Years* (Philadelphia-New York, 1962), p. 101.
38. "Alphonse Daudet," *Partial Portraits,* p. 207.
39. "Essays on French Literature: Feuillet," *Literary Reviews,* p. 177.
40. "Guy de Maupassant," *Partial,* pp. 258-259.
41. *Ibid.,* p. 285.
42. "Honoré de Balzac (1902)," *Notes on Novelists,* p. 142.
43. *Ibid.,* p. 120.
44. See "Honoré de Balzac," *French Poets,* p. 89.
45. *Loc. cit.*
46. *Loc. cit.*
47. *Ibid.,* p. 91.
48. "Flaubert," *Literary Reviews,* p. 150.
49. "Théophile Gautier," *French Poets,* p. 56.
50. "Charles Baudelaire," *French Poets,* p. 59. On this point, modern critics have sided with T. S. Eliot, rather than James. Eliot clearly distinguishes the genuine anguish of Baudelaire from the picturesque of Evil in Huysmans and Swinburne:

Huysmans . . . only succeeds in making his diabolism interesting when he treats it externally, when he is merely describing a manifestation of his period. . . . His own interest in such matters is, like his interest in Christianity, a petty affair. . . . But . . . Baudelaire is concerned, not with demons, black masses, and romantic blasphemy, but with the real problem of good and evil. . . . It is apparently Sin in the permanent Christian sense, that occupies the mind of Baudelaire. ("Baudelaire," *Selected Essays* [New York, 1950] pp. 378-379). Perhaps his only point of contact with James's impression is Eliot's assertion that Baudelaire's strength and sensibility are essentially passive.

Poe, too, is marked as an apostle of the picturesque of the mind, and as a charlatan, for all his genius. Baudelaire's admiration for him seems then, to James, only natural. It is interesting that Henry James, Sr., in an essay on Carlyle, objected to Carlyle's preference for the hero who is "picturesque" regardless of his moral stands. It is, perhaps, from his father that James inherited the pejorative usage of this term.
51. "Emerson," *Partial Portraits,* p. 31.
52. "Baudelaire," *French Poets,* p. 61.
53. *Ibid.,* pp. 61-62.
54. *Loc. cit.*

55. *Ibid.,* p. 64.

56. *Ibid.,* p. 65. Since James thought of an acted play as a "novel intensified" which "realizes what the novel suggests" ("The Parisian Stage," *The Scenic Art,* ed. Allan Wade [New Brunswick, 1948], p. 3), his comments upon the "picturesque" in the theater add a further dimension to the connection of felt life to felt art. In one of his critical dialogues James has his principal character object to a particular play because the "whole is a pictorial whole, not a dramatic one" ("After the Play," *Ibid.,* p. 231). In the great novels of James picture and drama feed each other, interacting like romance and the real. But when picture isolates itself from drama and becomes frozen into portrait, then it offers only a stultifying frame for the life of the characters. Isabel Archer must break through the portrait that Osmond wants only to see; Maggie Verver must activate the nun-nymph image which has fastened her; and Milly Theale's tragedy is that she cannot break away from the fixed picture of the dove to plunge into relationship.

If the isolated picturesque were elaborated in the novel, it, like the theater envisaged by James's spokesman, would "be at last a landscape without figures. I mean, of course, without figures that count" (*Ibid.,* p. 233). For James, a novel without figures that count is no novel at all. The split between picture and drama that is implicitly faced and combatted by James's greatest heroines is vividly reflected on the stage by the split between the art of utterance and the art of pantomime. After all, James's own characters are actors concerned with the deep fusion of word and deed——utterance in the art of acting is to pantomime as moral substance in the novel is to craft, or as the real is to romance. The pantomime in drama seems more easily mastered than utterance, but it is by itself less than an empty half. Ellen Terry, Irving, and Rossi are all in James's eyes picturesque artists who fail to plumb the depths of utterance and who, consequently, are in the second line of actors. To be picturesque without utterance is to lack moral depth. This is the implication of a typical complaint, out of James's dramatic criticism, against the "unintentional" school of pantomime. James is censuring Irving:

Of what the French call *diction*—the art of delivery—he has apparently not a suspicion. This forms three-fourths of an actor's obligations, and in Mr. Irving's acting these three-fourths are simply cancelled. What is left to him with the remaining fourth is to be "picturesque"; and this even his partisans admit he has made his specialty, . . . you cannot play Shakespeare by being simply picturesque. Above all, before all, for this purpose you must have the art of utterance. . . . ("The London Theaters," *ibid.,* pp. 104-105.)

57. See notes 39 and 40.

58. See "Henry James," *Literary Essays* (London, 1954), p. 303.

59. That James's critical concerns did not emerge *exnihilo* is fully attested by Richard Stang in *The Theory of the Novel in England, 1850-1870* (New York & London, 1959). Nevertheless, James's par-

ticular emphases, when seen as a body of assertions about the novel, put forth unique shapes and pressures.

60. *Partial Portraits,* p. 249.

61. *The Letters of Henry James,* ed. Percy Lubbock, I (London. 1920), 105.

62. *Partial Portraits,* p. 249.

63. "The Art of Fiction," *ibid.,* p. 379.

64. *Ibid.,* p. 380.

65. *Ibid.,* p. 379.

66. *Ibid.,* pp. 405-406.

67. "Trollope," *ibid.,* p. 124.

68. "Maupassant," *ibid.,* pp. 273-274.

69. *Ibid.,* p. 272.

70. *Essays in London,* p. 133.

71. "Robert Louis Stevenson," *Partial,* p. 144.

72. Preface to *The Princess Casamassima, The Art of the Novel,* p. 68.

73. Review of *"Middlemarch"* (1873) *The Future,* p. 89.

74. "The Life of George Eliot," *Partial,* p. 51.

75. *Ibid.,* p. 51.

76. *Letters,* I, 101.

77. "Eliot," *Partial Portraits,* p. 46.

78. "George Sand," *Notes on Novelists,* p. 196.

79. "Eliot," *Partial Portraits,* p. 52.

80. "The Novels of George Eliot," *Views and Reviews* (Boston, 1908), p. 33.

81. *Ibid.,* p. 36.

82. *Ibid.,* p. 37.

83. *Loc. cit.*

84. *Ibid.,* p. 32.

85. *Ibid.,* pp. 24-25.

86. *Ibid.,* p. 23.

87. "Daniel Deronda," *Partial Portraits,* p. 73.

88. *Ibid.,* p. 75.

89. *Ibid.,* pp. 78-79.

90. "Swinburne's Essays," *Views and Reviews,* p. 58.

91. *Ibid.,* p. 59.

92. "The Limitations of Dickens," *ibid.,* p. 159.

93. *Ibid.,* p. 160.

94. *Ibid.,* p. 161.

95. *Letters,* II, 266.

96. *Ibid.,* I, 225.

97. See Preface to *The American, The Art of the Novel,* p. 33.

98. "Zola," *Notes on Novelists,* p. 35.

99. "The Lesson of Balzac," *The Future,* pp. 113-114.

100. "Zola," *Notes on Novelists,* p. 36.

101. "Lesson of Balzac," *The Future,* p. 116.

102. *Letters*, I, 144.
103. "Balzac," *Notes on Novelists*, p. 152.
104. "Zola," *ibid.*, p. 30.
105. "Balzac," *ibid.*, p. 152.
106. *Letters*, II, 246.
107. "The New Novel," *Notes on Novelists*, p. 323.
108. "Zola," *ibid.*, p. 31.
109. "The New Novel," *ibid.*, p. 345.
110. *Ibid.*, p. 348.
111. *Letters*, I, 72-73.
112. *Ibid.*, pp. 30-1.
113. *Ibid.*, p. 167.
114. "Howell's 'A Foregone Conclusion,'" *Literary Reviews*, p. 214.
115. *The Eccentric Design* (New York, 1959), p. 239.
116. "The New Novel," *Notes on Novelists*, p. 317.
117. Preface to *The Portrait, The Art of the Novel*, p. 45.

Chapter III

1. D. H. Lawrence, "Morality and the Novel," *Phoenix*, p. 530.
2. See *Apocalypse* (New York, 1932) p. 196.
3. "Morality," *Phoenix*, p. 528.
4. See *The Sacred Fount* (New York, 1953), p. 260.
5. See *The Rainbow* (New York, 1927), p. 5.
6. "Morality," *Phoenix*, pp. 528 and 532.
7. "The New Novel," *Notes on Novelists*, p. 323.
8. *The Letters of D. H. Lawrence*, ed. Aldous Huxley (New York, 1932), p. 68.
9. *The Mirror of the Sea and A Personal Record*, ed. Morton Dauwen Zabel (New York, 1960), p. 267.
10. *Conrad's Prefaces*, ed. Edward Garnett (London, 1937), pp. 147-148.
11. *Notes on Life and Letters* (New York, 1921), p. 15.
12. "Morality," *Phoenix*, p. 530.
13. Lawrence, *Letters*, pp. 329-331.
14. "Morality," *Phoenix*, p. 531.
15. "The New Novel," *Notes on Novelists*, p. 318.
16. See D. H. Lawrence, *Psychoanalysis and the Unconscious* (New York, 1960), p. 46.
17. "A Propos of 'Lady Chatterley's Lover,'" *Sex, Literature, and Censorship*, ed. Harry T. Moore (New York, 1959), p. 106.
18. Lawrence, *Letters*, p. 294.
19. *Ibid.*, p. 413.
20. *Autobiography*, ed. Frederick Dupee (New York, 1956), p. 344.
21. *Ibid.*, pp. 338-339.
22. *Ibid.*, p. 340.
23. "Matilda Serão," *Notes on Novelists*, p. 300. One is always

reminded that James's strongest heritage comes from Jane Austen and George Eliot. He wanted to make that feminine sensibility count for the modern novel by turning away from the complacency of sociability and preconceived moral notions, and to make relationship itself determine morality. The old ghost of the picturesque is the stereotyped feminine sensibility, the kind that haunts the house of Pierre Loti:

> The closer, the more intimate is a personal relation the more we look in it for the human drama, the variations and complications, the note of responsibility for which we appeal in vain to the loves of the quadrupeds. Failing to satisfy us in this way such a relation is not, as Mr. Matthew Arnold says of American civilization, *interesting*. M. Pierre Loti is too often guilty of the simplicitiy of assuming that when exhibited on his own part it *is* interesting. (Henry James, "Pierre Loti," *Essays in London and Elsewhere* [London, 1893], p. 183.)

This kind of failure is neither Eliot's nor Austen's; theirs is at most a failure of freedom.

24. "Miss Prescott's 'Azarian,'" *Notes and Reviews,* p. 19.

25. *Ibid.,* p. 21.

26. *The Portrait,* II, 189.

27. *The Europeans* (London, 1952), p. 134.

28. *The Portrait,* II, 200.

29. Preface to *What Maisie Knew, The Art of the Novel,* p. 143.

30. Duration, constancy, and faithfulness to relationship are ranked as the highest Jamesian virtues by Joseph Warren Beach in his chapter on the "Ethics" of James in *The Method of Henry James* (New Haven, 1918).

31. Because of textual irregularities, all references to *The Ambassadors* will be to the Signet Classic Edition, ed. R. W. Stallman (New York, 1960). This phrase appears on p. 227. References to this novel immediately following will be noted in the text.

32. *The Portrait,* II, 433-434. References to *The Portrait* immediately following will be noted in the text.

33. For an illuminating discussion of Isabel's reasons for returning to Osmond see Dorothea Krook, pp. 357-362.

34. In a chapter concerning *The Portrait of a Lady,* in *The American Novel and Its Tradition* (New York, 1957), Richard Chase perceptively terms Isabel's persistent vision of life's experiences in abstractions "the romance of the self." Although many critics have discussed the romance of Isabel's vision, the best formal examination is still that of Dorothy Van Ghent in *The English Novel: Form and Function* (New York, 1953).

35. *The Ivory Tower* (New York, 1917), pp. 232-233.

36. *Ibid.,* p. 234.

37. Feodor Dostoievsky, *The Brothers Karamazov* (New York, 1950), p. 48.

38. *The American Scene* (New York, 1946), p. 458.

39. *The Wings of the Dove* (New York, 1907-9), I, 284. The references to this novel immediately following will be marked in the text.

40. This religious identification, as well as that of the Wagnerian and fairy tale themes are ably made and traced by Oscar Cargill, *"The Wings of the Dove,"* in *The Novels of Henry James* (New York, 1961).

41. *The Art of the Novel,* p. 297.

Chapter IV

1. Preface to *The Princess Casamassima, The Art of the Novel,* p. 68.

2. *Selected Essays* (New York, 1950), p. 111.

3. Preface to *The Princess, loc. cit.*

4. P. 19.

5. *The Art of the Novel,* pp. 128-129.

6. *Ibid.,* p. 78.

7. *Ibid.,* pp. 129-130.

8. *Ibid.,* p. 131.

9. *Loc. cit.*

10. *Notebooks of Henry James,* p. 248.

11. *Loc. cit.*

12. Preface to *Portrait, The Art of the Novel,* p. 48.

13. This aspect of the James heroine has been noticed by F. R. Leavis, *The Great Tradition* (New York, 1954), p. 123, and earlier by Yvor Winters's *Maule's Curse* (Norfolk, 1938), pp. 177-182.

14. Preface to *Portrait, The Art of the Novel,* pp. 49-50.

15. *Ibid.,* p. 51. It strikes the reader as unfair that F. R. Leavis, by paralleling some of James's own remarks on Eliot, can judge *Daniel Deronda* superior to *The Portrait of a Lady* largely on the grounds of Gwendolen Harleth's superiority to Isabel Archer. Gwendolen has, according to Leavis (*The Great Tradition,* p. 136 ff.), the advantage of specificity, moral thickness and fulness of vision. Though Leavis has many perceptive and appreciative things to say about James's method, he complains about James's requirement that the reader do "psychological detective work" from the outside in, instead of his giving us, himself, true "inward realization" of his characters. (This is basically a complaint about James's aesthetic emphasis.) But the two atmospheres are hardly comparable, and, as Leavis himself realizes, James deliberately simplifies social, economic, and, even moral density by allowing revelation to come through tested relationships, to be dramatically registered only by a "bewildered" consciousness. His fairy tale machinery, rather than fostering moral evasiveness, forces us to count unrelentingly on the individual case. It seems more rewarding and ultimately truer to insist on James's positive motivations rather than upon his failure to live up to an old form.

16. *Ibid.,* p. 55.

17. This famous phrase appears in the preface to *Princess, The Art of the Novel*, p. 66.

18. *Ibid.*, p. 67.

19. *The Golden Bowl* (New York, 1908-17), II, 236.

20. See "Maupassant," *Partial Portraits*, p. 285.

21. "Ivan Turgenieff," *ibid.*, p. 230. James here even equates the American and Russian heroines who share these qualities:

> . . . it does not seem too altogether fanciful to say that Russian young girls, as represented by Lisa, Tatania, Maria Alexandrovna, have to our sense a touch of the faintly acrid perfume of the New England temperament—a hint of Puritan angularity.

22. "George Eliot's *Middlemarch*," *The Future of the Novel*, ed. Edel, p. 83.

23. *Partial Portraits*, pp. 89-90.

24. *Views and Reviews*, pp. 20-21.

25. James, *Letters*, II, 254.

26. *Notes on Novelists*, p. 157.

27. *Ibid.*, pp. 76-77.

28. *Ibid.*, p. 83.

29. *Ibid.*, p. 84.

30. *Daniel Deronda*, II (New York, 1902), 426.

31. *The Portrait*, II, 414.

32. James, *Letters*, I, 101. One of the most interesting statements on consciousness that Henry James made, outside his critical prefaces, was an essay called "Is There a Life After Death?" (F. O. Matthiessen rescued this essay from oblivion and reprinted it in *The James Family* [New York, 1947].) The problem which James bravely attempts to resolve centers upon a reconciliation of the claims of consciousness and the hope for immortality. The attempt is not as successful as it is interesting, for it shows us that even in the immortal state, James saw himself as an artist devoted not to the extinction of consciousness, but to its extension. It is through the artistic process of creation itself that James becomes aware of the spiritual realm; the world of personality expands into a universe of potential relations. We feel that for James, the immortal state is only a quantitative enlargement of life's relational possibilities, rather than a qualitative correction of life's errors. The spiritual world is not for compensation but for intensification:

> I won't say that "the world," as we commonly refer to it, grows more attaching, but will say that the universe increasingly does, and that this makes us present at the enormous multiplication of our possible relations with it; relations still vague, no doubt, as undefined as they are uplifting, as they are inspiring, to think of, and on a scale beyond our actual use or application, yet filling us (through the "law" in question, the law that consciousness gives us immensities and imaginabilities wherever we direct it) with the unlimited vision of being. (p. 610)

We are not to be exposed in the after life to the unlimited vision of *non*-being. Matthiessen merely touches on a possible analogy between this conception, which was a late one (1910), and the growing emphasis upon a spiritual widening of consciousness and a loosening of that consciousness from social situation. Matthiessen springs too quickly into the ghost story. Yet the last lines of James's essay certainly evoke the image of Milly Theale's spirit which, in the novels, is the only great suggestion of the effect of an immortal influence upon the mortal remains of the living:

> And when once such a mental relation to the question as that begins to hover and settle, who shall say over what fields of experience, past and current, and what immensities of perception and yearning, it shall *not* spread the protection of its wings? No, no, no, —I reach beyond the laboratory-brain. (p. 614)

33. "Flaubert," *Notes on Novelists*, p. 85.

34. *Ibid.,* p. 85.

35. *Ibid.,* p. 87.

36. James, "Hardy's *Far from the Madding Crowd*," *Literary Reviews*, p. 297.

37. "Study of Thomas Hardy," *Phoenix*, p. 415.

38. Review of *Mastro-don Gesualdo, ibid.*, p. 227.

39. "Hardy," *ibid.*, p. 419.

40. *Ibid.,* pp. 419-420.

41. *Ibid.,* p. 480.

42. "Henry James," *Life and Letters*, p. 17.

43. *The Art of the Novel*, p. 5.

44. *Notes on Life and Letters*, pp. 17-18.

45. "Dante," *Three Philosophical Poets* (New York, 1910), p. 110.

46. A good example of the "new" defense of James on this point is the commentary of Geoffrey Tillotson, *Criticism and the Nineteenth Century* (London, 1951), p. 258.

47. *The Ordeal of Consciousness*, p. 369.

Chapter V

1. "George Sand," *Notes on Novelists*, p. 171.

2. "Gabriele D'Annunzio," *ibid.*, p. 292.

3. *Ibid.,* pp. 292-293.

4. *Ibid.,* p 276.

5. *Ibid.,* pp. 289-290.

6. D. H. Lawrence, "A Propos of 'Lady Chatterley's Lover,'" *Sex, Literature, and Censorship*, p. 100.

7. "D'Annunzio," *Notes on Novelists*, p. 282.

8. *Ibid.,* p. 284.

9. *Fantasia of the Unconscious* (New York, 1960), p. 220.

10. See "Matilde Serão," *Notes on Novelists*.

11. *Ibid.,* p. 310.

12. *Ibid.,* pp. 310-311.

13. "Sand," *ibid,* p. 222.

14. *The Wings of the Dove*, II, 216.
15. "Sand," *Notes on Novelists*, p. 171.
16. *Ibid.*, p. 179.
17. "Love," *Sex, Literature, and Censorship*, pp. 35-36.
18. *Notebooks*, p. 47.
19. I think it more profitable to treat the enforced innocence of the American heroine, which critics like Leslie Fiedler (Chapter 9 of *Love and Death in the American Novel* [New York, 1960]) see as a cultural deficiency of the American James (an interesting enough argument), as the essential objective metaphor for the dramatic foundation of the James novel.
20. "Sex versus Loveliness," *Sex, Literature, and Censorship*, p. 50.
21. *Phoenix*, p. 410.
22. *Ibid.*, p. 439.
23. *Ibid.*, p. 480.
24. *Ibid.*, p. 483.
25. *Ibid.*, p. 495.
26. *Ibid.*, p. 505.
27. *Aaron's Rod* (London, 1922), p. 96.
28. See Lawrence, *Letters*, p. 721.
29. "A Propos 'Lady Chatterley's Lover,' " *Sex, Literature, and Censorship*, p. 109.

Chapter VI

1. "Epictetus," *Notes and Reviews*, p. 181.
2. *Loc. cit.*
3. *Ibid.*, pp. 179-180.
4. *Ibid.*, pp. 180-181.
5. *Ibid.*, p. 181.
6. A review of "The Journal of Eugénie de Guérin," (Originally published in *The Nation*, December 14, 1865) *ibid.*, p. 122.
7. "The Lesson of Balzac," *The Future of the Novel*, p. 109.
8. See Review of "The Letters of Eugénie de Guérin," (Originally published in *The Nation*, September 13, 1866), *Notes and Reviews*, p. 210.
9. *The American Henry James*, p. 50.
10. "Can You Forgive Her," *Notes and Reviews*, p. 86.
11. *Partial Portraits*, p. 83.
12. *Ibid.*, p. 84.
13. "Maupassant," *ibid.*, p. 286.
14. "Dumas the Younger," *Notes on Novelists*, p. 372.
15. "Théophile Gautier," *French Poets and Novelists*, p. 46.
16. "Flaubert," *ibid.*, p. 201.
17. "Turgenieff," *ibid.*, p. 229.
18. "The Noble School of Fiction," *Notes and Reviews*, pp. 63-4.
19. *Ibid.*, p. 66.
20. Henry James, *Hawthorne* (London, 1902), pp. 50-51.

21. *Stories of Writers and Artists,* p. 21.
22. Hawthorne, p. 43.
23. "Emerson," *Partial Portraits,* p. 8.
24. *Roderick Hudson* (London, 1908), p. 32.
25. *Partial Portraits,* p. 13.
26. "The Madonna," *Stories,* p. 21.
27. *Notebooks,* p. 82.
28. *Hawthorne,* p. 45.
29. *Ibid.,* p. 58.
30. *Ibid.,* p. 58.
31. *The House of Fiction,* ed. Leon Edel (London, 1957), p. 186.
32. *Ibid.,* p. 180.
33. *Hawthorne,* p. 61. References immediately following will be given in the text.
34. "The Future of the Novel," *The Future,* p. 36.
35. "Maupassant," *Partial Portraits,* p. 287.
36. "The Future of the Novel," *The Future,* p. 38.
37. *Ibid.,* p. 37.
38. *Ibid.,* p. 39.
39. *Ibid.,* p. 41.
40. "Eliot," *Views and Reviews,* p. 24.
41. Henry James "The Lesson of Balzac," *The Future,* p. 116.
42. *Ibid.,* p. 98.
43. *The Art of the Novel,* p. 329.

Chapter VII

1. Notes to *The Ivory Tower* (New York, 1917), p. 303. Citations are to this edition.
2. "Miss Prescott's 'Azarian,'" *Notes and Reviews,* p. 21.
3. Wilson Follett, "The Simplicity of Henry James," *American Review,* I (May-June, 1923), 315-25; "Henry James's Portrait of Henry James," *New York Times Book Review* (August 23, 1936). Other articles of interest and intelligence are R. P. Blackmur, *The Sacred Fount, Kenyon Review,* IV (Autumn, 1942); Leon Edel, Introduction to the edition cited above; Robert A. Perlongo, *"The Sacred Fount:* Labyrinth or Parable," *Kenyon Review,* XXII (Summer, 1960). Newer contributions of James K. Folsom, "Archimago's Well: An Interpretation of *The Sacred Fount,*" *Modern Fiction Studies,* VII (Summer, 1961) and of Norma Phillips, *"The Sacred Fount:* The Narrator and the Vampires," *PMLA,* LXXVI (Sept., 1961), focus upon particular themes not stressed here. Oscar Cargill gives a good review of various attitudes in *The Novels of Henry James,* pp. 280-299.
4. *The Ordeal of Consciousness,* pp. 167-194.
5. For an excellent discussion of this technique see Wayne C. Booth, *The Rhetoric of Fiction* (Chicago, 1961), pp. 339-364.
6. Anderson, *The American,* ftnt. p. 222.

7. These terms appear in an unpublished letter of James to Mrs. Humphry Ward and are quoted by Leon Edel in his introduction to *The Sacred Fount* (New York, 1953,) p. xxx. Citations from *The Sacred Fount* in my text are to this same edition.

8. *The Art of the Novel*, p. 53.

9. "Daniel Deronda," *Partial Portraits*, p. 92.

10. *The Art of the Novel*, pp. 46-47.

Chapter VIII

1. Henry James, *The Golden Bowl*, New York edition (New York-London, 1908-1917), II, 298. Citations from *The Golden Bowl* in my text are to this edition. James had a fondness for this image of salvation. Compare *The Portrait*, II, 379.

2. In line with the carriage imagery, we might profitably turn to a compositional metaphor in the preface to *The Portrait of a Lady*. (*The Art of the Novel*, p. 55) in which James writes of the "ficelle" like Mrs. Assingham:

Maria Gostrey and Miss Stackpole then are cases, each, of the light *ficelle*, not of the true agent; they may run beside the coach "for all they are worth," they may cling to it till they are out of breath (as poor Miss Stackpole all so vividly does), but neither, all the while, so much as gets her foot on the step, neither ceases for a moment to tread the dusty road. Put it even that they are like the fish-wives who helped to bring back to Paris from Versailles, on that most ominous day of the first half of the French Revolution, the carriage of the royal family.

Chapter IX

1. Saul Bellow, *Henderson the Rain King* (New York, 1960), p. 300.

2. See *The Destructive Element* (Philadelphia, 1953).

3. An affirmation of the difference in direction between these class-oriented novels and the individual-oriented novels might emerge from the frequent references to "end" or "past" in the titles of the former.

4. "Attitudes toward Henry James," *Image and Idea* (Norfolk, 1949), p. 70.

5. *Anatomy of Criticism* (Princeton, 1957), Fourth Essay.

6. *Selected Letters*, p. 167.

7. In the epilogue of his excellent book *The Characters of Love* (New York, 1960), John Bayley makes interesting distinctions in this general area between the literature of "Nature" and that of "The Human Condition."

8. *Notes on Novelists*, p. 59.

9. "The Retreat from the Word," *Kenyon Review*, XXIII (Spring 1961), 189-216.

10. The phrase is William Troy's in "Scott Fitzgerald: The Au-

thority of Failure," *Forms of Modern Fiction,* ed. William Van O'Connor (Bloomington, 1959), p. 86.

11. F. R. Leavis gives a typical argument for the moral stand against Joyce's influence in *The Great Tradition,* p. 39.

12. For an interesting discussion of this point see Wayne C. Booth, "The Morality of Impersonal Narration," in *The Rhetoric of Fiction* (Chicago, 1961).

13. In *L'Ere du soupçon* (Paris, 1956).

14. "Our Hawthorne," *Partisan Review,* XXXI (Summer, 1964), 329-351.

15. D. H. Lawrence, *Letters,* pp. 199-200.

16. Norman Mailer, *The Deer Park* (New York, 1955), p. 375.

17. See especially the remarks of T. S. Eliot quoted and developed in Harry Levin, *James Joyce* (Norfolk, 1941), p. 134 and Joseph Frank, "Spatial Form in Modern Literature-I," *Sewanee Review,* LIII (April-June, 1945), 221-240.

18. For a stimulating discussion in this area see Wyndham Lewis, *Time and Western Man* (Boston, 1957). Georges Poulet, in his perceptive book *Studies in Human Time,* trans. Elliott Coleman (New York, 1956), makes an interesting, and I think valid distinction between Flaubert and James which would seem to contradict the assertion that James is a "temporal" novelist. The Jamesian novel takes place in the present and is divested of the past:

> Its characters undergo an infinity of experiences and incessantly discover themselves in new relationships with each other, but these experiences and relationships are oftenest the direct effect of present junctures; they are a new disposition of beings that corresponds to their displacement. An affair of the surface, and not one of depth; a movement in space, and not one in time. Ordinarily, the Jamesian character has little duration; or rather his duration is not composed, like that of the Flaubertian or Tolstoian character of a temporal density; between his immediate existence and the depths of his mind stretch no thick layers of memories. The duration of his characters is similar to the duration of celestial bodies; not that it is particularly long—rather the contrary—but it consists in the successive localization of a selfsame entity in different points of space. (p. 351)

It is obvious that Poulet is using "temporal" in a different light from ours. He is, actually, only insisting, and rightly so, on the metaphorical aspect of the Jamesian topography, in both space and time. As the Jamesian life is Present oriented (not determined) by nature of its innocence, the passage from America to Europe is most significant as a means of fulfilling the capacities of consciousness. Again, relationships, and the morality which they establish, are daily earned and daily renewed. They never, as do Flaubert's, "hang in the dusty rear."

19. "The Fact in Fiction," *Partisan Review,* XXVII (Summer, 1960), 438-458.

20. "Characters in Fiction," *Partisan Review,* XXVIII (Spring, 1961), 171-191.

21. In *The Liberal Imagination* (New York, 1953).

22. "Facts that Put Fancy to Flight," *New York Times Book Review,* February 11, 1962.

23. "The Novel Again," *Partisan Review,* XXIX (Spring, 1962), 171-195.

24. *Henderson the Rain King,* p. 156. All references of this novel in this chapter will be marked in the text.

25. *The Adventures of Augie March* (New York, 1953), p. 536.

Chapter X

1. "A Man Could Stand Up," *Parade's End* (New York, 1961), p. 544.

2. Ortega Y Gasset, *The Dehumanization of Art and Other Writings* (New York, 1956), originally translated in 1948.

3. *Autobiography,* pp. 157-158.

4. *A New Life* (New York, 1961), p. 360.

✑ List of Works Cited

Anderson, Quentin. *The American Henry James.* New Brunswick: Rutgers University Press, 1957.

Bayley, John. *The Characters of Love.* New York-London: Constable, 1960.

Bellow, Saul. *The Adventures of Augie March.* New York: The Viking Press, 1953.

———. *Henderson the Rain King.* New York: Popular Library Edition, 1960.

———. *Herzog.* New York: The Viking Press, 1964.

———. "Facts that Put Fancy to Flight," New York Times Book Review, 11 February, 1962.

Bewley, Marius. *The Eccentric Design.* New York: Columbia University Press, 1959.

Booth, Wayne C. *The Rhetoric of Fiction.* Chicago: University of Chicago Press, 1961.

Cargill, Oscar. *The Novels of Henry James.* New York: Macmillan, 1961.

Chase, Richard. *The American Novel and Its Tradition.* New York: Doubleday & Co., Inc., 1957.

Conrad, Joseph. *The Mirror of the Sea.* Garden City, N. Y.: Doubleday & Co., Inc., 1960.

———. *Notes on Life and Letters.* Garden City, N. Y. and Toronto: Doubleday, Page & Co., 1921.

———. *Conrad's Prefaces,* ed. Edward Garnett. London: J. M. Dent, 1937.

Dostoievsky, Feodor. *The Brothers Karamazov.* New York: The Modern Library, 1950.

Edel, Leon. *Henry James: The Middle Years.* Philadelphia: Lippincott, 1962.

Eliot, George. *Daniel Deronda.* 2 vols. New York: P. F. Collier & Son, 1902.

Fiedler, Leslie. *Love and Death in the American Novel.* New York: Criterion Books, 1960.

Flaubert, Gustave. *The Selected Letters of Flaubert,* ed. Francis Steegmuller. New York: Farrar, Straus and Cudahy, 1953.

Ford, Ford Madox. "A Man Could Stand Up," *Parade's End.* New York: A. A. Knopf, 1961.

Frank, Joseph. "Spatial Form in Modern Literature-I," *Sewanee Review,* LIII, (April-June, 1945) 221-240.

Frye, Northrop. *Anatomy of Criticism.* Princeton: Princeton University Press, 1957.

Howe, Irving. *Politics and the Novel.* New York: Meridian Books, 1957.

James, Henry. *The Ambassadors.* New York: The New American Library, 1960.

————. *The American Scene.* New York: C. Scribner's Sons, 1946.

————. *The Art of the Novel,* ed. R. P. Blackmur. New York: Scribner's Sons, 1934.

————. *Autobiography,* ed. Frederick Dupee. New York: Criterion Books, Inc., 1956.

————. *The Bostonians,* Introduction by Lionel Trilling. London: Chiltern Library, 1953.

————. *The Bostonians,* Introduction by Irving Howe. New York: Modern Library, 1956.

————. *Essays in London and Elsewhere.* London: J. R. Osgood, McIlvaine & Co., 1893.

————. *The Europeans.* London: John Lehmann, 1952.

————. *French Poets and Novelists.* London: Macmillan & Co., 1908.

————. *The Future of the Novel,* ed. Leon Edel. New York: Vintage Books, 1956.

————. *Hawthorne.* London: Macmillan & Co., 1902.

————. *The House of Fiction,* ed. Leon Edel. London: Rupert Hart-Davis, 1957.

————. *The Ivory Tower.* New York: C. Scribner's Sons, 1917.

————. *The Letters of Henry James,* ed. Percy Lubbock. 2 vols. London: C. Scribner's Sons, 1920.

————. *Literary Reviews and Essays,* ed. Albert Mordell. New York: Twayne Publishers, 1957.

————. The New York Edition of the Novels. New York-London: Macmillan, 1908-1917.

————. *The Notebooks of Henry James,* ed. F. O. Matthiessen and K. B. Murdock. New York: Oxford University Press, 1955.

————. *Notes on Novelists.* New York: C. Scribner's Sons, 1914.

————. *Notes and Reviews,* ed. Pierre de Chaignon la Rose. Cambridge, Mass.: Dunster House, 1921.

————. *Partial Portraits.* London: Macmillan & Co., 1911.

————. *The Sacred Fount.* New York: Grove Press, 1953.

————. *The Scenic Art,* ed. Allan Wade. New Brunswick: Rutgers University Press, 1948.

————. *Stories of Writers and Artists,* ed. F. O. Matthiessen. Norfolk: New Directions, 1949.

————. *Views and Reviews.* Boston: The Ball Publishing Co., 1908.

Keats, John. *The Selected Letters,* ed. Lionel Trilling. New York: Doubleday & Co., Inc., 1956.

Krook, Dorothea. *The Ordeal of Consciousness in Henry James.* Cambridge: Cambridge University Press, 1962.

Lawrence, D. H. *Aaron's Rod.* London: Martin Secker, 1922.

————. *Apocalypse.* New York: The Viking Press, 1932.

————. *The Letters of D. H. Lawrence,* ed. Aldous Huxley. New York: The Viking Press, 1932.

————. *Phoenix.* London: Heinemann, 1936.

————. *Psychoanalysis and the Unconscious* and *Fantasia of the Unconscious.* New York: Viking Press, 1960.

————. *The Rainbow.* New York: The Modern Library, 1927.

————. *Sex, Literature, and Censorship,* ed. Harry T. Moore. New York: The Viking Press, 1959.

Leavis, F. R. *The Great Tradition.* New York: Doubleday & Co., Inc., 1954.

————. Preface to *Selected Literary Criticism of Henry James,* ed. Morris Shapira. London: Heinemann, 1963.

Levin, Harry. *James Joyce.* Norfolk: New Directions, 1941.

Lewis, Wyndham. *Time and Western Man.* Boston: Beacon Press, 1957.

Mailer, Norman. *The Deer Park.* New York: G. P. Putnam's Sons, 1955.

Malamud, Bernard. *A New Life.* New York: Farrar, Straus and Cudahy, 1961.

Marcus, Steven. "The Novel Again," *Partisan Review,* XXIX (Spring, 1962), 171-195.

Matthiessen, F. O. *The James Family.* New York: A. A. Knopf, 1947.

McCarthy, Mary. "The Fact in Fiction," *Partisan Review* (Summer, 1960), 438-458.

————. "Characters in Fiction," *Partisan Review* (Spring, 1961), 171-191.

O'Connor, Frank. *The Mirror in the Roadway.* New York: A. A. Knopf, 1956.

Ortega Y Gasset. *The Dehumanization of Art and Other Writings.* New York: Doubleday & Co., Inc., 1956.

Poulet, Georges. *Studies in Human Time,* trans. Elliott Coleman. New York: Harper & Brothers, 1956.

Pound, Ezra. *Literary Essays,* ed. T. S. Eliot. London: Faber & Faber Limited, 1954.

Rahv, Philip. *Image and Idea.* Norfolk: New Directions, 1949.

Santayana, George. *Three Philosophical Poets.* New York: Doubleday & Co., Inc., 1910.

———. *Character and Opinion in the United States.* New York: Doubleday & Co., Inc., 1956.

Sarraute, Nathalie. *L'Ere du Soupçon.* Paris: Gallimard, 1956.

Spender, Stephen. *The Destructive Element.* Philadelphia: A. Saifer, 1953.

Stang, Richard. *The Theory of the Novel in England, 1850-1870.* New York-London: Columbia University Press, 1959.

Steiner, George. "The Retreat from the Word," *Kenyon Review,* XXIII (Spring, 1961), 187-216.

Tillotson, Geoffrey. *Criticism and the Nineteenth Century.* London: Athlone Press, 1951.

Trilling, Lionel. *The Liberal Imagination.* New York: Doubleday & Co., Inc., 1953.

———. *The Opposing Self.* New York: The Viking Press, 1955.

Troy, William. "Scott Fitzgerald: The Authority of Failure," *Forms of Modern Fiction,* ed. William Van O'Connor. Bloomington: University of Indiana Press, 1959.

Van Ghent, Dorothy. *The English Novel: Form and Function.* New York: Harper & Brothers, 1953.

Warren, Austin. *Rage for Order.* Ann Arbor: University of Michigan Press, 1948.

Wegelin, Christof. *The Image of Europe in Henry James.* Dallas: Southern Methodist University Press, 1958.

Wells, H. G. *Boon,* in *Henry James and H. G. Wells,* ed. Leon Edel and Gordon N. Ray. Urbana: University of Illinois Press, 1958.

Winters, Yvor. *In Defense of Reason.* Denver: Alan Swallow, 1947.

———. "Problems for the Modern Critic of Literature," *Hudson Review,* IX (Autumn, 1956), 325-386.

ᴥ§ Index

The manuscript was edited by Mary Garner and the book was designed by Richard Kinney. The text type face is Intertype Garamond based on the design cut by Jean Jannon about 1615. The display type face is Garamont based on the same source.

The book is printed on S. D. Warren's Olde Style, white wove paper and bound in Bancroft's Arrestox B cloth over boards. Manufactured in the United States of America.